LATINO
SOCIAL
MOVEMENTS

LATINO SOCIAL MOVEMENTS

HISTORICAL AND THEORETICAL PERSPECTIVES

A *NEW POLITICAL SCIENCE* READER

RODOLFO D. TORRES AND GEORGE KATSIAFICAS, editors

ROUTLEDGE
New York and London

Published in 1999 by
Routledge
29 West 35th Street
New York, NY 10001

Published in Great Britain in 1999 by
Routledge
11 New Fetter Lane
London EC4P 4EE

Library of Congress Cataloging-in-Publication Data

Latino social movements : historical and theoretical perspectives /
    a new political science reader
    edited by Rodolfo D. Torres and George Katsiaficas.
            p.   cm.
    Includes bibliographical references and index.
    ISBN 0–415–92299–2 (pbk.)
        1. Hispanic Americans—Politics and government. 2. Hispanic Americans—Social conditions. 3. Hispanic Americans—Economic conditions. I. Torres, Rodolfo D., 1949–   .
II. Katsiaficas, George N., 1949–   .
        E184.S75L3636   1999   98–33289
        305.868—dc21   CIP

                    10 9 8 7 6 5 4 3 2 1

Contents

Rodolfo D. Torres and George Katsiaficas

INTRODUCTION

> *Over the past several decades, Latinos in the United States have emerged as strategic actors in major processes of social transformation. This new reality— the Latinization of the United States—is driven by forces that extend well beyond U.S. borders and asserts itself demographically and politically, in the workplace and in daily life.*[1]

We are pleased to publish this anthology devoted to contemporary Latino politics in the United States. Latinos are an increasingly important segment of the population and have emerged as a major force in the United States, yet this diverse population seldom receives the attention merited by its size or significance. In an earlier publication of some of these articles as a special issue of *New Political Science,* we noted that the growing Latino presence is closely intertwined with transnational economic forces that are restructuring and reshaping once familiar local, regional, national, and international landscapes. In four decades, global political-economic changes have greatly stimulated Latino immigration to the United States. From a mere 4 million in 1950, accounting for only 2.7 percent of the nation's population, Latinos increased more than fivefold to 21.1 million, or 8.5 percent of the total population, in 1990. The Latino population is now growing at the rate of 900,000 persons a year, including net immigration of 350.000. It is estimated that there are now nearly 29 million Latino Americans, or 11 percent of the total U.S. population. According to recent Census Bureau figures, Latinos will supplant African Americans as the nation's second largest minority by the year 2005. By the year 2050, it is projected, Latinos will outnumber all other minority groups combined. According to the Census Bureau, California is now 30 percent Latino and could have a Latino majority by the year 2040.

More important than sheer numbers is the fact that Latinos are a significant and growing sector of the United States' working class. Within a few years, Latinos will make up more than a quarter of the nation's total workforce, a percentage that is more than three times out of proportion to their numbers in the population. Equally important, Latino men and women are increasingly concentrated in the very industries and areas that have been most influenced by the economic restructuring of the United States. Los Angeles County, for example, is the post-industrial heartland of the United States, with industries based on low-paid, nonunionized workers drawn increasingly from the ranks of immigrants, both legal and undocumented. The county is also the nation's largest manufacturing center, with 711,000 workers employed in manufacturing. Nearly half of these workers are Latinos. If present employment trends continue, Los Angeles's industrial workforce will be almost completely Latinized within several decades.

In spite of Latinos' numbers and growing importance, the ongoing Latinization of manufacturing employment over the last several decades has drawn scant notice from scholars, except for some occasional superficial commentaries. The lack of scholarly attention may be attributed to several factors. Perhaps some public policy analysts underestimate the significance of Latino workers because of a tendency to view them as a marginalized sector of the working class. Hence the ubiquitous (and erroneous) perception that the majority of Latina/o workers are employed primarily as farm laborers. Another reason for a lack of attention is the failure of scholars to come to terms with the political and socioeconomic consequences of postindustrial society. Given the strategic space occupied by Latinos in the United States, it is imperative that scholars develop a conceptual language for understanding new forms of racialized relations in a rapidly changing political economy.[2] Needless to say, this will require a radical break with the dominant race-relations paradigm, which assigns analytical status to the idea of race and frames "racial" matters in terms of black and white.[3] As noted by Valle and Torres, much needs to be learned about the nature and meaning of Latino class relations in a postindustrial society and the manner in which these divisions manifest themselves in the emerging organization of work, urban politics, and relations with the state.[4] This class diversity and different historical experiences within the immigrant population make representing them as a single group highly problematic.

Latino immigrants are connected to their native countries by transnational economic and social processes. The economic conditions faced by Latino communities in the United States are linked to the same international reality shared by populations of Latinos in Latin America and the Caribbean, despite specific regional histories that give rise to particular sociocultural configurations. These configurations are shaped within the context of the ever-changing global economy, the fundamental force that determines migration, production relations, and class positions. The current socioeconomic conditions of Latinos can be directly traced to the relentless expansion of the global economy, most recently exemplified by economic policies such as the North American Free Trade Agreement. NAFTA has weakened the labor participation of Latinos through the transfer of historically well-paying manufacturing jobs to Mexico and other "cheap labor" manufacturing centers around the world. Such a consequence highlights the need for scholars to link the condition of U.S. Latinos to the global economy.

The study of social, cultural, economic, and political changes in the conditions of Latinos must occur in the context of the particular role that Latinos, as a racialized group, have played in the economic system. As William Robinson noted:

> Much sociological writing on Latino groups has focused on demographic phenomena, language, culture, and other descriptive or ascriptive traits. Other studies have stressed emerging ethnic consciousness, pan-Latino political action, and other subjective factors as causal explanations in minority group formation. These factors are all significant. However, in my view, there are broad, historic "structural linkages"

among the distinct groups that constitute the material basis and provide the underlying causal explanation for Latino minority group formation. In other words, cultural and political determinations are relevant, but subsidiary, in that they only become "operationalized" through structural determinants rooted in the U.S. political economy and in an historic process of capital accumulation into which Latinos share a distinct mode of incorporation.[5]

In light of this perspective, Latino politics can only be fully understood and adequately theorized within the context of the U.S. political economy and the international division of labor.

The United States is the wealthiest country in the world today, yet it is the country with the greatest economic inequality between the rich and the poor and with the most disproportionate wealth distribution of all the "developed" nations of the world. To overlook these facts in the analysis of Latino politics would be to ignore the most compelling social phenomenon in the U.S. social structure—the growing class inequality. That such an analysis is needed is underscored by the recent tendency in postmodern and poststructural studies of Chicano/Latino culture (and society as a whole) to slight and even dismiss the importance of class, capital, patriarchy, and labor as analytic categories. With their emphasis on discontinuity, fragmentation, difference, and rejection of master narratives (which means, ultimately, a denial of history), many partisans of postmodernism have conceptualized away capitalism and patriarchy as objects of analysis.[6] The globalization of capital and changes in class relations form the very groundwork of contemporary Latino politics and cultural formations but are conspicuously absent in most contemporary postmodern accounts of Latino life in the United States—accounts that ignore the increasing significance of class and the specificity of global capitalism as the system underlying social and political relations of power. The contributors to this volume challenge such accounts and place labor, class, patriarchy, and capital at the center of their analysis.

The intersection of these objective realities with the subjective context of popular attempts to transform the existing conditions of life is the unifying theme of the articles gathered in this anthology. The chief preoccupation of the esteemed group of contributors we have assembled is to analyze social movements. Although their theoretical perspectives are quite varied, they grapple with the relationship of race, gender, class, and ethnicity. These issues (or issue, depending upon one's perspectives) are vitally important to the theoretical understanding of the resistance to global political economy, national political power, and regional social structure. We do not seek to arrive at a simple answer to the question of how these different levels of being are related. By juxtaposing this question with the experiences of several social movements, we hope to dramatize real-life answers to the questions, thereby clarifying theoretical concerns while simultaneously demonstrating the centrality of social movements to our understanding of the essential character of society.

This is an optimistic collection of essays by writers/activists/teachers who see themselves as analyzing the past in order to prepare for future engagement aimed at conscious social transformation. As opposed to the irrational imperative of corporate decision making based upon profitability, we advocate structuring society in accordance with the human needs of the vast majority of people. Our authors do not come to a uniform agreement on what can or should be done. Where Luis Aponte-Parés leans toward the need for autonomy of Puerto Rican groups, Martha Gimenez grounds her analysis in the commonality of class interests, and Teresa Córdova's main concern is the aspirations of Chicanas. This seeming inconsistency reflects the current multifarious character of contemporary thinking on race, gender, and class.

Moreover, many analyses have been about Puerto Ricans or Chicanos, but not both groups simultaneously. Central to our understanding of society is the importance of social movements in shifting identities. Nowhere is this clearer than in the relatively recent emergence of the category "Latinos" as the appropriate way to understand so many disparate peoples. Over the past twenty years, we have witnessed a remarkable blending of what were formerly separate identities into a Latino consciousness that grew out of the social movements we discuss. There have yet been few attempts to compile a diverse anthology related to Latino social movements. Previously published studies have been internally coherent. In his twenty-year-old classic, *Race and Class in the Southwest,* Mario Barrerra conceptualized Chicanos as a class-differentiated and racialized population. His theoretical contribution lay in defining, locating, and connecting the subordinate class position of Chicanos with institutionalized patterns of discrimination and the interests of capital. This book remains critical to understanding Latino politics in the age of globalization. Ten years ago, Carlos Muñoz Jr. related the Chicano movement to the global movements of the 1960s. In a new major study of social movements in Los Angeles, Mary S. Pardo provides a much-needed class analysis as well as gender focus on Chicana activists and political struggle within the context of growing income inequality and social polarization.[7]

Our collection begins with "Anti-Colonial Chicana Feminism," by Teresa Córdova. Her paper is an overview of Chicana writings since 1991 and provides a guide to this burgeoning field. After outlining a history of Chicanas in universities and the explosion of their intellectual output, she looks within, emphasizing the pain, recovery, and celebration expressed by Chicana writers and confronting the impact of "internalized colonialism," which influences relations among Chicanas. For Córdova, the greatest potential value of Chicana feminist writing, especially certain lesbian writing, is "speaking secrets" to challenge the structure of power. Significantly, she retains the motion of the collective good as relevant to the project of Chicana feminists.

In "Lessons from *el Barrio*—The East Harlem Real Great Society/Urban Planning Studio: A Puerto Rican Chapter in the Fight for Urban Self-Determination," Luis Aponte-Parés provides an invaluable analysis of a chapter in the Puerto Rico struggle for autonomy. Taking as his point of departure the 1960s in the Lower East Side and in East Harlem, Aponte examines a year in the life of the East Harlem Real Great Society/Urban Planning Studio. RGS/UPS emerged during a transition period in the development of Puerto Rican institutions, and its staff's eagerness to speak for the needs and aspirations of Puerto Ricans was a clear example of an ethnicity-based struggle. Although grounded in an ethnic-specific realm, Aponte examines class, gender, and racial dynamics among Puerto Ricans, African Americans, and whites in his study of this important episode of resistance in New York City. His analysis is concerned with the history of what transpired both *within* contested terrains as well as *between* them and the powers that be.

Victor Rodriguez's article, "Boricuas, African Americans, and Chicanos in the 'Far West': Notes on the Puerto Rican Pro-Independence Movement in California, 1960s–1980s," explores alliances that Puerto Rican activists made with a variety of people—Chicanos, African Americans, Chileans, and whites. From the late 1960s through the 1980s Puerto Ricans developed a movement in California in support of the island's movement for political independence. Their alliances extended the influence of the movements in solidarity with Puerto Rico's struggle beyond the relatively small and geographically dispersed Puerto Rican population in California. Political alliances led to a vital ideological and cultural exchange between radical Puerto Rican organizations and other groups. Rodriguez's focus is on those who were in positions of leadership and influence in San Francisco and Los Angeles within the radical circles of the Puerto Rican Socialist Party, which at that time was the main Puerto Rican socialist organization in Puerto Rico and the United States.

In "The 1933 Los Angeles County Farm Workers Strike," Gilbert González reconstructs Chicano political history and reveals that the Mexican governments in the post-1910 revolutionary era implemented a strategy to influence the political culture and actions of the emigrant community in the United States. Significantly, during the strike (the largest in the history of California agriculture to that date), official representatives of Mexico in California acted in concert with U.S. police to intervene against Communist labor organizers. Gonzalez conclusively demonstrates that the Mexican community in California not only acted in relation to conditions within the United States, but also reacted to their home government, which followed them across the border in an attempt to assimilate them into the social relations and political culture of Mexico. The Mexican state aimed at nothing less than developing a loyal and politically dependent emigrant community, a strategy that replicated Mexico's domestic social policy and complemented both Roosevelt's New Deal labor objectives and the demands for cheap labor made by large-scale agricultural interests.

Edna Bonacich continues the focus on Los Angeles with a contemporary view of Latino immigrant workers in the Los Angeles apparel industry. She considers the return of sweatshops based on the large Latino workforce, many of whom are undocumented. For her, the fundamental problem lies in the lack of political power of these workers, who must labor under an apartheidlike system that denies them basic civil rights. Bonacich carefully enumerates the advantages of subcontracting for manufacturers in the postmodern apparel industry. One study she cites shows that more than half (61 percent) of all southern California firms in this sector failed to pay even the federally mandated minimum wage to their workers. In conjunction with the fact that in Los Angeles Latinos are at least 43 percent of the population but only 15 percent of the electorate, Bonacich reveals the brutal contours of a contemporary form of segregation. She concludes by discussing current unionization efforts, particularly within one of the main beneficiaries of the brutal exploitation in the apparel industry, Guess? Inc.

Martha Gimenez reflects on the future of Latino politics and class struggle. She begins by articulating a critique of contemporary categories of race, particularly the term *Hispanic,* which she understands as imposed from above by bureaucratic fiat. For Giminez, all politics built around an identity presupposes the reality of that identity. She examines the structural and ideological barriers to Latino identity formation and the structural commonalities that shape the experiences conducive

to Latino identity formation. Her main argument is that preferences for and debates about ethnic labels/identities and ethnic
claims often mask class divisions and class-based grievances
within this population.

While most of our analysts have avoided electoral politics,
Richard Santillan takes up this theme in his analysis of La Raza
Unida Party, an alternative to the Anglo-dominated mainstream
Democratic and Republican parties in Texas. Partisanly advo-
cating Chicano nationalism, La Raza Unida Party emerged in
southern Texas in the 1960s. It espoused the need for an
autonomous Chicano political system with its own democrati-
cally elected, self-governing congress. All too often, La Raza
Unida Party is a forgotten chapter in the histories of third parties in the United States, and we hope that people involved with
the current revival of interest in third parties will take note of
the history included here.

Notes

1. Frank Bonilla, "Changing the Americans from Within the United
   States," in *Borderless Borders: U.S. Latinos, Latin Americans, and the
   Paradox of Interdependence*, edited by Frank Bonilla et al.
   (Philadelphia: Temple University Press, 1998).

2 See Antonia Darder and Rodolfo D. Torres, "The Politics of 'Race'
   Language in 'Postmodern' Education," in *The Promise of
   Multiculturalism: Education and Autonomy in the 21st Century*, edited
   by George Katsiaficas and Teodros Kiros (New York: Routledge, 1998).

3. See Neil Foley's brilliant new comparative study, *The White Scourge:
   Mexicans, Blacks, and Poor Whites in Texas Cotton Culture* (Berkeley:
   University of California Press, 1997). This timely and award-winning
   study provides a fertile source of new ideas in political economy, social
   history, and cultural studies. Foley does a masterful job of treating with
   analytical rigor the multiplicities of racialized relations.

4. Victor Valle and Rodolfo D. Torres, "Latinos in a 'Post-Industrial'
   Disorder," *Socialist Review*, vol. 23, no. 4 (1994), pp. 1–28.

5. William Robinson, "The Global Economy and Latino Populations in
   the United States: A World System Approach," *Critical Sociology*
   (1993), pp. 29–30.

6. For a critical reading of the postmodern project and fashionable trends of "post-Marxism" that reject class analysis, see *Democracy Against Capitalism: Renewing Historical Materialism,* by Ellen Meiksins Wood (Cambridge University Press, 1995). For a critique of postmodernism's failure to deal with feminist concerns, see Seyla Benhabib, *Situating the Self: Gender, Community and Postmodernism in Contemporary Ethics* (New York: Routledge, 1992).

7. See Mario Barrerra, *Race and Class in the Southwest* (Notre Dame, IN: University of Notre Dame Press, 1979); Carlos Muñoz Jr., *Youth, Identity, Power* (London: Verso, 1989); and Mary S. Pardo, *Mexican American Women Activists: Identity and Resistance in Two Los Angeles Communities* (Philadelphia: Temple University Press, 1998).

Teresa Córdova
University of New Mexico

Anti-Colonial Chicana Feminism

Abstract *During the 1980s and 1990s, a critical mass of Chicana feminist scholars established a space and a voice to express an identity of opposition. This paper is an overview of Chicana Studies writings since 1991, emphasizing the pain, recovery, and celebration expressed by Chicana writers. In addition, and perhaps most importantly, I discuss the anti-patriarchal, anti-colonial challenges posed by Chicana theorists and feminists. I also confront the impacts of "internalized colonialism" that influence relations among Chicanas. Finally, I pose questions about the future writing agendas of Chicana feminists. An examination of Chicana feminist writings reveals the anti-colonial features of her process of recovery and survival. The greatest potential value of Chicana feminist writing, especially certain lesbian writing, is "speaking secrets" to challenge the structure of power, the colonial patriarchy, and our participation in perpetuating it. The "collective good" continues as a dream and as a goal for the anti-colonial Chicana feminist.*

Colonialism has imbedded its memory in our spirits. After stripping us of our institutions, our resources, and our history, the colonizer asserts his superiority and declares us deficient and deserving of our own fate.[1] The usurper "extols" himself at our expense. The indelible mark of shame and inferiority is one of colonialism's most effective tools. The history of the Chicana feminist writer involves her fight for recovery and survival from the "memory of molestation,"[2] from the "penetration" by those who tell her she is not good enough. She is finding her voice to express her pain and her experiences, to rename herself in her own image, to recover mythic and historical female symbols

0739–3148/98/040379–19 © 1998 Caucus for a New Political Science

that reconnect her to her past, and to celebrate and learn to love herself. The Chicana feminist writer reconstructs her self to liberate it from the oppression of the colonialist construct whose only purpose is to debase her in order to control her.

An examination of Chicana feminist writings reveals their *anti-colonial* features. By reclaiming self and space, Chicanas counter colonialism, which I define as the "taking over" of someone else's space by a dominant power who then expropriates its resources. Those who must live in "occupied" land are burdened with the constant struggle for survival—culturally, spiritually, and economically. The extent to which Chicana writers are *anti-colonial* varies, often as a function of how they view themselves in relation to the colonizer. There are writers, nonetheless, whose *anti-colonial* position poses critical challenges against a key ideological basis of colonialism—patriarchy. The potential value of the most critical Chicana feminist theory is the fundamental challenge to the orderings of power. Who, then, are these writers and how is their work *anti-colonial?*

During the 1970s and mid-1980s, a critical mass of working-class Chicanas filtered through the walls of the ivory towers of American universities. We conveyed our experiences through essays, poetry, literature, and even social science. We named ourselves *femenistas,* and our complex experiences, the "intersections of class, race, and gender."[3] We struggled, not only to survive the elitist university, but to recover ourselves from the treacherous conditions of racism and patriarchal domination. Yet, despite the rich history of resistance, the struggles of Chicana feminist writers are far from ended, a testament to the enduring legacies of colonization and to the contemporary realities of *re-colonization.*[4]

This paper is a continuation of "Roots and Resistance: The Emergent Writings of Twenty Years of Chicana Feminist Struggle."[5] In this paper, I continue to overview Chicana Studies writings since 1991, emphasizing the pain, recovery, and celebration expressed by Chicana writers. In addition, and perhaps most importantly, I discuss the anti-patriarchal, anti-colonial challenges posed by Chicana theorists and feminists. At the same time, I confront the impacts of "internalized colonialism" that influence relations among Chicanas. Finally, I pose questions about the future writing agendas of Chicana feminists.

Revisiting "Roots and Resistance"[6]
"Roots and Resistance" was about breaking silence through the written word.

> Chicana feminists have struggled to find their voices— have struggled to be heard. Our struggles continue but our silence is forever broken. We are telling our stories and we are recording our triumphs and, by virtue of our presence, we are challenging our surroundings.[7]

During the late 1960s and 1970s, Chicanas wrote about the issues affecting their working-class communities: employment issues, labor struggles, education, child care, prisoner rights, sterilization, legal rights, health, welfare rights, birth control, images of women, and sex roles. They also wrote about their emerging identity as *femenistas*.[8] Instead of yielding to the demands for silence, Chicanas declared the existence and legitimacy of a Chicana feminism significant to the Chicano movement and distinct from white feminism.

Between 1975 and 1981, Chicanas added to their poetry, literature, and autobiographical testimonies and continued to write about feminism. Social issues remained a theme as the writings of this period were a logical and political extension of the previous one. More elaborate analyses and research characterized these works. The writings established four major points: (1) the Chicana is not inherently passive—nor is she what the stereotypes say she is; (2) she has a history rooted in a legacy of struggle; (3) her history and her contemporary experiences can only be understood in the context of a race and class analysis; and (4) the Chicana is in the best position to describe and define her own reality. The starting point was the rejection of traditional image and the debunking of social science myths about the Chicana. The result was the redefinition of the Chicana—by the Chicana.

In the early 1980s, a critical mass of Chicanas in universities organized to assert their agenda in the National Association for Chicano Studies (NACS). In 1982, members of Mujeres en Marcha, from the University of California, Berkeley, sponsored a panel to raise the issues of sexism in the organization.[9] The following year we organized the Chicana caucus and called for the next conference theme to be *Voces de la Mujer*. The 1984 conference centered on the work of women and resulted in the volume, *Chicana Voices: Intersections of Class, Race, and Gender*.[10] The volume is an important reminder of the emergence of the Chicana scholar to take her rightful place within academia. The Association continues to be an important mechanism for interaction among professors, students, and community. As a result of insistence by Chicana activists within the organization, the name is now The National Association for Chicana and Chicano Studies (NACCS).

At approximately the same time that Chicanas were asserting our presence within NACS, we established a Chicana Studies organization, *Mujeres Activas en Letras y Cambio Social* (MALCS). MALCS continues to meet annually and produces a *Journal of Chicana/Latina Studies*.[11] The rich Preamble of MALCS conveys the values of the working-class Chicanas who viewed their work in universities as intertwined with their connections to their communities:

> We are the daughters of working class families involved in higher education...Our research strives to bridge the gap between intellectual work and active commitment to our communities. We draw upon a tradition of political struggle. We see ourselves developing strategies for social change—a change emanating from our communities.

During the 1980s, extensive writings within Chicana Studies included history and social science research that demonstrated the ways in which Chicanas are active agents in their work and home. Again, labor struggles, labor force participation, images and myths, health and mental health, and immigration were among the topics researched by Chicana writers. In addition, literature, poetry, and autobiographical testimonies flourished. These writings explored border consciousness and the *mestiza;* connections to family, especially *abuelitas* and mothers; struggles with relationships; sexuality; and of course, the pains of racism.

These writers expose the truth of their pain to such a degree that it is no longer possible to ignore the significance of the impact of oppression on the individual. The writings of Chicanas remind us that not only is the personal political, but when they express their experiences so deeply, the personal is profound. It is these experiences that form the basis of new theories and methodologies that more accurately reflect what happens in the so-called margins. The new theories challenge the dominant culture's interpretation of the experiences of women of color and set the stage for a total reconsideration of all dominant theory, including dominant feminist theory.

The very articulation of the Chicana reality through her own voice is immediately, by its very nature, a voice of resistance and the foundation for "oppositional consciousness."[12] To speak is to oppose. To give voice to emotions is to expose the sham of complicity. The act of deconstructing and reconstructing Chicana images is a subversive move against years of ideological mistreatment. What Chicanas speak is a function of their experiences. To speak about those experiences is to find themselves in opposition with those that would define them otherwise. The result, as evident in the writings of Chicana feminists, is an *identity of opposition.*

Chicanas write in opposition to the symbolic representations of the Chicana movement that did not include them. Chicanas write in opposition to hegemonic feminist discourse that places gender as a variable separate from that of race and class. Chicanas write in opposition to academics, whether mainstream or postmodern, who have never fully recognized them as subjects, as active agents. The very essence of Chicana writings is to establish Chicanas as subjects and to replace all previous representations with self-representations. The act of redefining the experiences of Chicanas through their own voices is an expression of resistance against all other definitions. When Chicanas confront hegemonic representations they question the symbolic bases of power relationships. The expression from the margins is a fundamental challenge to the orderings of power.

Chicana Studies in the 1990s
Chicana Studies, therefore, was born out of resistance. The critical mass of Chicana feminist scholars established a space and a voice, *un sitio y lengua,* to express our *identity of opposition.* We created our organization (MALCS), Chicana and lesbian caucuses within NACCS, a body of writings and research that constitutes the "field" of Chicana Studies, a *Chicana Studies Journal,* and several academic positions. Since 1992, Chicanas published several anthologies of feminist writings. In 1992, the University of New Mexico Press reprinted *Chicana Voices: Intersections of Class, Race, and Gender.* An updated foreword describes why the essays in the volume are still relevant and includes an analysis of the activities of Chicanas within NACCS since the original publication in 1986.[13] MALCS published *Chicana Critical Issues* and Pesquera and de la Torre edited *Building with Our Hands: New Directions in Chicana Studies,* both in 1993. *Perspectives in Mexican American Studies* featured a special issue on Chicanas.[14] Alma Garcia edited *Chicana Feminist Thought: Basic Historical Writings* and, most recently, Carla Trujillo edited a volume called *Living Chicana Theory.*

Poetry, Literature, and Autobiography from 1992–1997
Literary works by Chicanas exploded in the 1990s. The many novels, short stories, autobiographies, and books of poetry include: Emma Pérez's *Gulf Dreams* (1996); Pat Mora's book of essays *Nepantla* (1993); Demetria Martinez's *Mother Tongue* (1994); Norma Cantu's *Canícula: Snapshots of a Girlhood en la Frontera* (1995); Mary Helen Ponce's *Hoyt Street* (1993); Ana Castillo's *So Far From God* (1993); Alicia Gaspar de Alba's *The Mystery of Survival and Other Stories* (1993); *El Milagro and Other*

Stories (1995); Helena Maria Viramontes' novel, *Under the Feet of Jesus* (1995); Denise Chavez's novel, *Face of an Angel* (1994); Sandra Cisneros' *Loose Woman* (1994); Cherrie Moraga's *The Last Generation* (1993); Lucha Corpi's mystery *Eulogy for a Brown Angel;* Alma Villanueva's novel *Naked Ladies* and a collection of short stories, *Weeping Woman: La Llorana and Other Short Stories* (1994); Estella Portillo Trambley's fiction, *Rain of Scorpions and Other Stories;* Carmen Tafolla's book of poetry, *Sonnets to Human Beings and Other Selected Works;* poetry by Gloria L. Velasquez in *Superwoman Chicana* (1997); and a host of other writers who publish in an array of collections and chap books.

In addition, several anthologies were published which compiled the creative works of Chicana, and in some cases Latina, writers: Lillian Castillo-Speed's *Latina: Women's Voices from the Borderlands* (1995); Roberta Fernandez's *In Other Words: Literature by Latinas of the United States* (1994); and Diana Rebolledo and Eliana Rivero's *Infinite Divisions* (1993). Literary criticism included Rebolledo's *Women Singing in the Snow* (1995) and María Herrera-Sobek and Helena María Viramontes' *Chicana Creativity and Criticism: New Frontier in American Literature, Second Edition* (1996).

The power of the Chicana writer is in the strength and beauty of her voice. Chicana writers are telling their stories of pain, recovery, and triumph. By making herself the subject of her own writings, the Chicana writer of the 1990s continues to assert the authority of representing herself through the use of symbolic imagery drawn from her own cultural meaning and experiences. Writing from those experiences, "the Chicana writer finds that the self she seeks to define and love is not merely an individual self, but a collective one. In other words, the power, the permission, the authority to tell stories about herself and other Chicanas comes from her cultural, racial/ethnic and linguistic community."[15] These stories are rich and rewarding, especially for the Chicana herself, who is seeking to retrieve the self-love that colonialism and patriarchy attempt to strip from her. The themes of Chicana writings are numerous. The limits of this paper allow me to mention only a few.

The pain of various forms of oppression continues as a theme during the 1990s. Alicia Gaspar de Alba writes about the runaway slave in her short story, "Cimarrona."[16] Using vivid imagery and a reconstructed historical memory of slavery and bondage (including rape), she tells the story of resistance and the search to escape "destiny." Implicit in her story is the message of how love and loyalty between women can provide the strength and courage to find freedom. "She was sobbing, now, choking on the humors of the sea, fighting the current like a netted fish until at last, she felt her head break through the surface, and her face came up and she swallowed air."[17]

Emma Pérez, in her literary expression of the need to break from the "addiction to patriarchy," writes about repressed and distorted desire in her novel *Gulf Dreams*.[18] She juxtaposes repressed desire of lesbian love with the tyranny of patriarchal rape. The novel's protagonist obsesses in her search to fulfill the "erotic and pure" dreams of a young girl that become distorted by a patriarchal system that punishes those who speak against it. Speaking out destroys while it liberates. Patriarchal abuse taints the search for passion and desire. Sometimes the way out is not so easy, leaving us few choices to cross the line towards liberation.

As Chicanas seek their own liberation, they identify closely with struggles of their Central American sisters. In doing so, the Chicana writer sees herself connected to the collective concerns for survival. The courts, for example, convicted Demetria Martinez, and then later acquitted her on First Amendment grounds, of "smuggling" Central American refugees into the United States. Naomi Quiñónez asks:

> Does the sun still shine in El Salvador
> where echoes of murdered children
> run the width and breadth of rifle barrels?[19]

Carmen Tafolla, in her poem "In Guatemala," writes of the horrors of torture and brutality in Guatemala brought on by "government officers":

only Ixil Indians in rebellion
their red woven messages of humanness
in whole Indian villages corralled, beheaded,
for existing too full
of straight-backed human dignity[20]

Cherrie Moraga, also struck by the horrors of U.S. policies in Central America, states in her book of essays, *The Last Generation,* that she does not side with George Bush's interference with the Nicaraguan Revolution, nor the Republican Latinos who support him. She emphatically states what she considers her role to be as an artist:

> As a Latina artist, I can choose to contribute to the development of a docile generation of would-be Republican "Hispanics" loyal to the United States or to the creation of a force of "disloyal" *americanos* who subscribe to a multicultural, multilingual, radical restructuring of American. Revolution is not only won by numbers, but by visionaries. And if artists aren't visionaries, then we have no business doing what we do.[21]

The Chicana writer moves quickly from pain to recovery and resistance. Resurrecting ancestral memory, connecting to indigenous roots, retrieving legend and oral tradition, returning to spirituality, and controlling self-representation are mechanisms by which Chicana writers recover and resist. Several writers express their connections to *abuelitas* and traditional ways. Demetria Martinez, in her novel *Mother Tongue,* writes about food and the old *remedios:*

> Now remember, food is the best medicine. All this depression going around—it's because we've gotten too far away from the foods of our ancestors. And our cells never forget. Beans, rice, avocado, cilantro, etc. We must make every effort to eat what our elders

ate, eat with the seasons, and eat what is grown nearby. All these newfangled drugs aggravate illness but
hide the symptoms. No wonder we're all crazy.[22]

An important dimension of *El Movimiento* was the acknowl-
edgement that, as Chicanos, we were products of conquest and
colonization. The reconnection to indigenous roots continues
to be an important element of Chicana consciousness. Through
spiritual practice such as *danza* Chicanas are retrieving their
souls and healing the wounds of the colonized memory. Ana
Castillo continues her "search of identity" in her book of essays,
Massacre of the Dreamers. She retrieves the feminine principle
that the masculine construction of pre-Hispanic mythology
subsumed, and then reconstructs the "Mexic Amerindian
women":

> All early societies seem to yield traces of Mother wor-
> ship. The Mexica did as well. Tonantzin, Mother
> Earth, was worshipped on hills and mountains.
> Iztachihuatl, the volcano near Pueblo, was another
> version of Her. But by the time we get to the sixteenth
> century, the militant Mexica had transformed
> Coatlicue (another version of the Mother) into a
> ghastly, hostile deity.[23]

In the 1990s, Chicana writers continue redefining legendary and
mythic figures: Coatlicue, La Malinche, La Virgen de
Guadalupe, La llorona, Sor Juana Inez de la Cruz. In *Women
Singing in the Snow*, for example, Rebolledo describes poetry
and literature that builds on the power of these mythic figures
to recreate them as sources of strength and inspiration.[24]
Anzaldúa developed her concept of border consciousness
through her reliance on a *mestiza* consciousness provided by the
image of Coatlicue.[25] Angie Chabram Dernersesian describes
how Chicana cultural producers are "reclaiming a subject position" by reconfiguring images of Malinche and La Virgin.[26]
Alicia Gaspar de Alba brings to life the character of Sor Juana

Ines de la Cruz. Made easier by the legacy of her writings, Gaspar de Alba resurrects the person of Sor Juana, who is able, in her own words, to come alive as an intellect and a lover of women. Her choice to be a nun was preferable to a "compulsory heterosexuality" that would condemn her to patriarchal submission. The highly creative interview with Sor Juana is an excerpt from Gaspar de Alba's forthcoming novel on Sor Juana.[27]

Chicanas also turn to spirituality and tradition as they seek refuge and recovery from colonization. As Lara Medina states in her article on Chicana Spiritualities,

> The spiritual practices of many Chicanas emerge from a purposeful integration of their creative inner resources and the diverse cultural influences that feed their souls and their psyches. Accepting their estrangement from Christianity, whether Protestant or Catholic (and their wounded souls), many Christians (re)turn to an *indigena*-inspired spirituality, learn to trust their own senses and bodies, recreate traditional cultural practices, and look to non-Western philosophies—all of which offer us a (re)connection to our selves, our spirits, and of the ongoing process of creating *nuestra familia*. As they journey on paths previously prohibited by patriarchal religions, Chicanas define and decide for themselves what images, rituals, myths, and deities nourish and give expression to their deepest values.[28]

Chicanas are drawing upon their spirituality to find healing through ceremony and ritual. This spiritual work, says Medina, enables women to "take control of their lives." Through ritual, woman can develop their abilities to assume leadership and authority.

Chicana cultural critics are directly confronting popular culture images in film and art and many cultural producers are replacing these images with self-representations of identity. The formation of Chicana identities is a creative dynamic process. Chicana cultural producers, according to Angie Chabram Dernersesian, have played the significant role of replacing unfavorable presentations with ones that more adequately portray the complexity of Chicana identity.

> They altered the subject position of Chicanas in cultural productions, taking them from subjection to subjectivity, from entrapment to liberation, and from distortion and/or censure to self-awareness and definition.[29]

The self-representation of the Chicana, she argues, remains an important site of resistance, where Chicanas can create discourses of who they are to more accurately reflect the dignity they deserve, a dignity that Chicanas do not easily obtain.

Rosa Linda Fregoso demonstrates how even Chicano filmmakers are continuing to portray Chicanas in stereotypical and negative ways.[30] The "mother motif," she states, is prevalent and depicted in such a way as to reproduce the dominant discourse. Yet, as Marta Cotera reminds us, Chicanas have been challenging constructs of women and resisting the "patriarchal virtues" of the corrido since a time that precedes Americo Paredes, but were "simply ignored or silenced."[31] Chicana writers continue to insist on redefining Chicana identities in opposition to the images created by others as mechanisms to make her invisible, irrelevant, or indecent.

Celebration and Self-Love

The triumph for the Chicana writer is reaching a state of self-love. If the fundamental outcome of colonized identity is self-hatred, then the Chicana who can achieve self-love is closer to her liberation. In her processes of healing and recovery, the Chicana feminist searches for the acceptance of her self as she attempts to erode the negative messages of a colonized memory. Chicana lesbian feminist theory is especially powerful in its potential. The message they impart is the beauty of women loving women—as women. By extension, we should be able to love ourselves—free from the need to obtain patriarchal approval. The challenge to patriarchal authority over our psyches is tied to the anti-colonialist position against repressive domination.

History and Social Science Writings: Intersections of Class, Race, Gender, Sexuality, and Colonialism

Yvette Flores-Ortiz, a psychologist, attests to the significance of issues of self-love and the power of patriarchal domination in "Voices from the Couch."[32] Through her practice as clinician, Flores-Ortiz describes the importance of a Chicana psychology. She stresses the importance of being aware of culture and political context in shaping a Chicana identity.

In her work on domestic violence, for example, she offers a "model of analysis and treatment for Raza families" to replace approaches that blame Latino culture by ignoring issues of cultural freezing, the impacts of colonization, and racism.[33] The myth of martyrdom, for example, contributes to the Chicana's identity with respect to violence. Religious and cultural icons (e.g. La Virgin and Malinche) influence women to find valor in being "self-sacrificing, self-effacing, long-suffering martyrs." "Guided by these cultural 'mandates,' women often feel that it is their lot in life to suffer."[34] In her recommendations for approaches to treatment, she urges us to consider the significance of the "legacies of colonialism." "Having access to one's history, understanding the facts and how these impact individual and family health, provides women with tools to fight the 'isms.'"[35]

Chicana historians are retrieving some of our historical memory to enable us to recover more effectively from the pains of the past. Antonia Castañeda conveys in her article, "Sexual Violence in the Politics and Policies of Conquest," the connection between the frequent rape of the Indian woman and mechanisms of subordination during centuries of colonial rule.

[T]he sexual and other violence toward Amerindian women in California can best be understood as ideologically justified violence institutionalized in the structures and relations of conquest initiated in the fifteenth century. In California as elsewhere, sexual violence functioned as an institutionalized mechanism for ensuring subordination and compliance. It was one instrument of sociopolitical terrorism and control.[36]

Castaneda researches women historically by looking "at the intersecting dynamics of gender, race, culture, class, and sexuality in the politics, policies, structures, and relations of conquest and social development in frontier California."[37] Thus, in addition to the soldiers, priests, and settlers who played roles in the brutalities of the conquest, she also examines the relations among women and their functions in frontier Spanish society. In "Presidarias y Pobladoras," she demonstrates how women of various class positions employed mechanisms to promote or challenge the gender construction of colonial rule and "assert their own prerogatives or power."

Deena Gonzalez, another historian, retrieves the image of La Tules (Dona Gertrudis Barcelo) from the Euro-American construct that defined her as a woman of loose morals.[38] Gonzalez reconstructs Santa Fe in the 1840s and depicts the racist and stereotypical portrayal of La Tules that by extension was applied to other Mexican women, who were "debased in all moral sense." Yet the numerous accounts of La Tules missed the point.

> If she existed on the fringes of a society, it was because she chose to place herself there—a woman with enormous foresight who pushed against her own community's barriers and risked being labeled by the travelers a madam or a whore.[39]

The image of La Tules is especially significant in light of the historical period during which Protestant men seeking fame and fortune overwhelmed the region. Their presence signaled the encroachment of Euro-Americans and the rise of racial and cultural conflict. La Tules exemplified the confrontation between "independent female Catholics" and "westering male Protestants." She also represents one strategy of accommodation and resistance in the face of the Americanization of the region. She ran a saloon with gambling and she positioned herself so that many sought her advice, often "travelers."

> Yet in giving herself to the conquest, but not the con-querors, she survived and succeeded. She drew bet-ting clients to her saloon; they played but lost, she gambled and won. In the end, the saloon that attract-ed conquerors released men who had been con-quered.[40]

It is the pain of the present, however, that keeps the historical memory fresh. Reminders of racist exploitation of our labor, the unequal and inadequate access to social services, toxic contam-ination, and expropriation of local resources are all issues that continue to impact the Chicana and her families. Chicana Studies scholars trained in the social sciences are conducting research that profiles various Chicana populations. Mary Romero, in her book on both paid and non-paid domestic workers, discusses the historical emergence of domestic labor-ers, and the dilemmas of class issues between middle-class women and domestic laborers.[41] Elisa Facio conveys aspects of the world of Chicana elderly and describes the important func-tion of senior citizen centers in replacing the household as a basis for community.[42] Pesquera writes about the *political strug-gle* over household labor and the interplay between expectations of women of different class backgrounds and the actual behav-ior with respect to the distribution of work.[43] Adela de la Torre describes the "Hard Choices and Changing Roles among Mexican Migrant *Campesinas*" and how gender inequality in capitalist development impacts conditions and characteristics of migrant work.[44] Marta Lopez-Garza studies informal labor among Central American and Mexican women in L.A. and how they are creating "spaces" in which they merge their private

household work with their public wage work.[45] Patricia Zavella
continues her work on cannery workers to discuss the strategies
used to organize them.[46] Many of these descriptions emphasize
the ways in which Chicanas are active agents in their work,
home, and communities, a theme that continues from previous
social science writings.

Several Chicana Studies scholars are also conducting policy related research in the area of alcohol use, adolescent female
behavior, education, law, and public health. María Alaníz, for
example, studies targeted advertising by alcohol companies and
shows how it commodifies historical and cultural symbols, uses
sexist images, and affects community norms and behaviors. In
addition, she and her research team have demonstrated the
direct relationship of the density of alcohol advertising in communities and violence against Latinas in those communities.
They determined that the connection between alcohol advertising and availability with violence was statistically significant.[47]
What makes this research additionally interesting is the "community based research" approach that involves community
members in every phase of the project, especially the question
formulation stage.[48]

Juana Mora continues her work on alcohol consumption
patterns among Chicanas. She also examines the cultural competence of treatment programs and local environmental ways of
reducing alcohol abuse.[49] She is involved in several policy making bodies and advocacy groups at the local and national level.
Elena Flores examines issues of preadolescent female sexuality.
Numerous professors of education, law, mental health, and
public health also publish in their fields on issues related to
Chicanas.

Chicanas have documented the resistance efforts of Chicana
activists, especially labor organizers.[50] The examples of unrecord-
ed labor activism, however, are countless, leaving room in the
Chicana Studies literature for more accounts of historical and
contemporary efforts. Cynthia Orozco writes on the participation
of women within LULAC, a civic organization.[51] Chicanas have
written about involvement of Chicanas/Mexicanas in social

movements showing that Chicanas/Mexicanas are critical actors in fights for social justice. They have, nonetheless, also fought within their organizations on issues of how the men treat the women.[52] There are even fewer written documentations of Chicana activism that is community or neighborhood based. Mary Pardo's research on the "Mothers of East L.A." describes their fight against an incinerator and a prison in their neighborhood. Pardo points out that in their organizing, the Mexicanas turned their preexisting gender based networks into political benefits; bringing forward previously "invisible" women into leadership positions; transforming the identity of "mother" into a force for political opposition; developing their own cultural and political identities; and developing a sense of entitlement on behalf of their communities.

In my article on Chicana grassroots organizers in the Environmental Justice Movement, I characterize the work of the Southwest Organizing Project. These Chicanas display a sophisticated knowledge base including an understanding of socioeconomic conditions and their causes; function with a high level of "oppositional consciousness" and a sense of the "collective good"; engage in principled strategies designed to directly confront the logic of their opposition; work in coalition with other groups but still maintain a specific cultural and regional identity; and as gender conscious Chicanas, utilize organizations that are not gender based to impact issues facing their communities.[53]

> [G]rassroots activists are inserting themselves into questions of international economic integration, local economic development, neighborhood change including issues of gentrification, infrastructure, tax abatements, natural resource management, zoning, and an array of other development issues. The potential of these activities and this social movement are enormous, as grassroots organizations define questions of social change as their realm in their struggle for environmental and economic justice.[54]

The work of grassroots organizers alerts us to the many issues facing Chicanas. Corporate welfare is replacing social welfare. The gap is increasing between the rich and the poor, with Latinos continuing to comprise the largest segment of the working poor. Labor force segmentation enhances the concentration of Chicanas/Mexicans in low wage employment often under toxic working conditions. Rates of certain diseases increase while access to adequate health care, housing, and education erode. Communities are experiencing impacts of displacement, contamination, and depletion of natural resources. Chicana activists express their views on these issues through newsletters, magazines, correspondence, and newspaper editorials.[55] The fundamental challenge posed by these activists is the challenge against patriarchal power expressed through corporate power.

Chicana Feminist Theory: Challenging Patriarchy, Challenging Power Relations

One of the most important potential implications of Chicana feminist theory is the articulation of an *anti-colonial* challenge against patriarchal power—the power of conquest. Chicana feminism is the break from patriarchal power. One of the most significant aspects of Chicana feminist theory is the role that lesbians have played in its leadership and development. In the now classic piece, Emma Pérez makes the connection between conquest, patriarchal power, and the significance of the challenge to sociosexual relations. This requires a stand against the perpetrator/victim dynamic that prevents the realization of collective work for the common good.[56]

Drawing upon male psychoanalytic theory (Freud, Lacan, and Foucault) to describe male behavior and French feminist critics of those theories (Cixous, Duras, Irigaray), Pérez brings in the elements of race, class, and culture to deconstruct patriarchal ideology within colonization. Pérez reevaluates the Oedipal complex, the point when men realize their sociosexual power, and describes what she calls the "Oedipal-Conquest-Complex." This "conquest triangle" is only one part of the puzzle to understand why Chicanas "uphold the law of the white-colonizer European father, knowing the extent of damage and pain for Chicanas and Chicanos."[57] Pérez finds the answer in the perpetrator/victim dynamic that for women begins with "the molestation memory," the point when "girls realize that they do not have sociosexual power in relation to men."[58] The result is an "addiction" to patriarchy where one fears "violating the father's orders" and where an entire social structure betrays her if she refuses to succumb to patriarchal mandates.

Luis Valdez symbolizes this relationship in his theatre production *Corridos*—a decision Pérez asserts reveals his male-centrist anxieties and "eroticizes women's victimization." The story of "Delgadina" shows a young woman who has refused the advances of her father, is placed in a tower without food or water and eventually dies. Despite her pleas to her mother, sister, and brother, "Each one fears violating the father's order, his sexual laws, so they each ostracize Delgadina."[59]

> The song tells us about a young woman's death when she challenges the sexual law of the father. She cannot, however, break from the law, happy and free to join with women who believe her, or a community who will allow her to be. There is no such community. Instead, a male-centralist society with male-identified women cannot even hear her language, her pain. They just know they cannot defy the father.[60]

The incestuous language and behavior were already operating by the time the father commands Delgadina to allow his "penetration." According to Pérez, that "penetration" was not necessary to create "a memory of molestation" that enters her psyche and leaves the pain of inappropriate behavior that goes unchallenged—by anyone.

> Like Delgadina, women live in this cycle of addiction/dependency to the patriarchy that has ruled women since the precise historical moment that they

become aware that women's bodies are sexually
desired and/or overpowered by the penis.[61]

This "memory of molestation" may result in repudiation of the
molester but often "victims continue to repudiate and embrace
the perpetrator in a persistent pattern through relationships
until that addictive/dependent cycle is broken."[62] The answer,
argues Pérez, is to "resist the perpetrator" in order to abandon
"phallocentric law and order." Letting go of capitalist patriarchal
notions of sexual law and order is necessary in order to create a
collective in the common good: "social sexual relations between
men and women condoned by the patriarchy are inherently
unhealthy and destructive most of the time."[63]

Pérez is concerned with fundamental social change and
believes that it is impossible without fundamentally challenging
the social sexual ideology of patriarchy. Chicanas defy this patriarchy when they can find "a specific moment of consciousness
when they can separate from the law of the father into their own
sitio y lengua. The writings of women of color, according to
Pérez, emerge from a space and language that "rejects colonial
ideology and the by-products of colonialism and capitalist
patriarchy—sexism, racism, homophobia, etc."[64]

Chela Sandoval agrees:

> Any social order that is hierarchically organized into
> relations of domination and subordination creates
> particular subject positions within which the subor-
> dinated can legitimately function. These subject
> positions, once self-consciously recognized by their
> inhabitants, can become transformed into more
> effective sites of resistance to the current ordering of
> power relations.[65]

Chicana writings, therefore, are representations of resistance.
The separation from domination through authority makes possible the break from the perpetrator/victim cycle. As Chicanas
join in alliance with women of color, they are looking to extend

their resistance to forge effective opposition to all forms of domination for the "collective good." Chicana feminism, from this perspective, is not anti-male. The purpose of Chicana feminism is not to bring down men in order to bring up women, but to bring down patriarchy, in the interest of the collective good, the community. The men *and women* who support patriarchy are obstacles to the collective good.

In a more recent article, Pérez suggests the importance of *strategic essentialism* as a significant location and discourse from which to challenge powers of domination.[66] Firmly situating herself in her own identity as a Chicana lesbian and a "historical materialist from the Southwest who dares to have a feminist vision of the future," she rejects the attacks

> by a carload of postmodern, post-Enlightenment, Eurocentric men and by women who ride in the back seat, who scream epithets at those of us who have no choice but to essentialize ourselves strategically and politically against dominant ideologies that serve only to disempower and depoliticize marginalized minorities.[67]

It is by *strategic essentializing* that we are able to create an important practice against the hegemonic ideologies that define us in ways to silence us and control us. *Strategic essentializing,* she argues, is a powerful way to find the decolonized spaces among ourselves. It does not provide a final destination, but a journey by which we may find our "multiple identities" so necessary in the fight against colonization. It is the fight for social change that most compels Pérez to argue for our own self-definitions and our own decolonizing spaces.

In "Power and Knowledge: Colonialism in the Academy," I begin with the premise that breaking silence against oppression is an important anti-colonial act because silence and compliance are so critical to maintaining exploitative relationships.[68] Chicana feminism is the move away from silence, giving voice to our experience. Yet more significantly, "Chicana feminism is the refusal to participate in colonial activity." To assess whether an identity is an anti-colonial, therefore, is more than whether it is an identity of race, class, gender, and sexuality. The question is what is one's *identity toward power?*

What is one's position in relation to the colonial patriarch? What is the role that one plays in the mix of colonial relations? Does one function, for example, as an overseer, imposter, or wimp? Is one doing the dirty work of the colonizer when obsessively seeking the approval of the colonizer by helping to obtain the compliance or to punish the defiance of one's own? After analyzing an array of colonial relations and how they function in relation to power, I speak of the importance of self-love as a counter to dehumanization, a fundamental aspect of colonizing forces. I then stress the importance of a *discourse of resistance* in which I say,

> We cannot allow the colonizer, or those who serve him/her, to define what is appropriate resistance, for s/he shall always tell us to behave. They do the most outrageous things and then tell us how we are supposed to react to them.[69]

Speaking "truth to power," borrowing a Malcolm X phrase, remains a significant *anti-colonial* act. Internal colonialism and adherence to patriarchal ideology compel many of us to perpetuate and participate in colonial activity. Exposing the dynamics of that betrayal is an important message of this paper. Other Chicana writers are doing just that.

Deena González agrees that "speaking secrets" is an important mechanism to stop the abuse that goes on when we do not.[70] In her bold articulations of the many "differences" turned nasty, Gonzalez exposes the degree to which Chicana and Chicano academics attempt to interfere with and destroy the careers of "out" lesbian Chicanas. They do so because they are so desperately fearful of those they call the "lesbian terrorists," those who are not afraid to name the most insidious power games among us. They reject those who most fundamentally challenge the ideology and structure of patriarchy. In the attempt to erase the significance of Chicana lesbian warriors among us, we learn instead about the misogyny that still permeates academic culture. González's purpose in speaking so openly is so that we can "deal with these issues" and "break the cycle of violence." To do so

> means that we must begin to name our fears, to acknowledge that we cannot move forward alone, and that each step we take to tell secrets moves us one step closer toward...liberatory, transformative life.[71]

Is "speaking secrets" necessarily a move toward liberation? Was Luis Valdez "speaking secrets" when he dramatized the attempted incest by the father in his *Corrido* on Delgadina? Does it matter how we tell those secrets? Does eroticizing the incest challenge the power around which that incest is based? According to Pérez, it does not. Rather, it condones it. "Speaking secrets," therefore, would seem to be about "breaking cycles of violence," and requires "speaking truth to power." We "speak secrets" to challenge the foundations of capitalist patriarchy—the political, economic structure of power that enables the worst of male dominance to prevail.

Nearly all Chicana feminist writings speak of the importance of giving voice to our experiences and the need to define those experiences. They also speak of recovery and find healing in traditions, icons, and spirituality. The self-love that Chicana writers seek serves as a counter to the dehumanizing impacts of colonization, which is one of its most effective tools. Yet, the greatest potential value of Chicana feminist writing, especially some lesbian writing, is "speaking secrets" to challenge the structure of power, the colonial patriarchy, and our participation in perpetuating it. Finding "decolonized spaces" helps us to do this.

Thoughts for Chicana Studies
This paper characterizes aspects of the writings of Chicanas who entered universities in the 1970s and 1980s and formed

enough of a critical mass to believe we could establish a space for ourselves within the academy. Every aspect of that endeavor is a struggle. Academia is a difficult place to survive, let alone thrive, particularly given its features of a colonial institution.[72] The struggles are apparent in our writings. Nonetheless, we have made significant strides, not the least of which is the creation of the field of Chicana Studies. In establishing our Chicana Studies organization, MALCS, we recognized our "scarcity" in institutions of higher education and we knew that we needed to join together "to identify our common problems, to support each other and to define collective solutions." Our purpose, we claimed, was to fight the oppression we experienced and to "reject the separation of academic scholarship and community involvement."

The spoken secrets, however, suggest that the "differences" among us have not always meant support for one another nor the ability to define collective solutions. Our different *identities toward power* have meant that we battle against one another on issues of whether to challenge the patriarchal power structure. Some of us have stood alongside the colonizer and have helped him against the forces of rebellion. Some of us do not even believe that Chicano and Chicana Studies should be based in "dinosaur ideologies of the past" that call for a connection to our communities. Some of us do not even think about "community" because our worlds have become so intertwined away from it.

Meanwhile, as we struggle for our positions within the university, the women of our communities are facing increased labor segmentation and poor working conditions, toxic contamination and deteriorating health, increased incarceration and addiction of our male children, and so on. The increasing internationalization of economies and politics has meant the increasing exploitation of women of color worldwide, including Chicanas and Mexicanas. Where is Chicana Studies? What are Chicana Studies scholars doing to address these issues? What is the purpose of our research and writing?

The Chicana Studies scholar is concerned with research "rooted in the political life of communities" and rejects "the separation of academic scholarship and community involve-ment." According to the Preamble of MALCS, "We document, analyze, and interpret the Chicana/Mexicana experience" and see ourselves "developing strategies for social change—change emanating from our communities.... We continue our moth-ers' struggle for social and economic justice." How does the Chicana scholar collaborate in developing strategies for social change as she conducts her research? Who is the Chicana schol-ar in relation to those she "studies"? How can a Chicana schol-ar avoid reproducing colonial treatments of research "subjects" and, instead, contribute to questions of social change? Are we really developing new methodologies? What are the criteria for academic integrity for the Chicana scholar concerned with questions of social and economic justice?

These and many others are some of the questions we have yet to adequately ask ourselves, let alone answer. And while many of our writings are *anti-colonial*, many are not. While many challenge the essence of domination and oppression, many perpetuate it. Granted, our lives in the university are dif-ficult, but they are also privileged. When do the explorations of our selves become self-indulgent; when are they truly *anti-colonial?*

There is still much work to be done. When we entered the university, we entered with a sense that we were part of a movement, that others had struggled for us to be there. Many of us still continue with that sense of responsibility that requires us to make our work in the university useful. Undoubtedly, a great number of us contribute through our mentoring with students, many of whom are working-class Raza looking for someone to whom they can relate. Undoubtedly, a great number of us contribute through our research that replaces otherwise racist depictions of our expe-riences. But if we are not tying either our teaching or our research to the needs of our communities, and if we are per-petuating oppressive relations through our colonized and col-onizing politics, then can we really say that we are doing enough? Can we really say that our work is *anti-colonial?*

For many, the dream is still very much alive for our work to have relevance in the larger struggle against the forces of exploitation that continue to keep many of our people suffering. The "collective good" continues as a dream and as a goal for the *anti-colonial* Chicana feminist who "speaks secrets" from her decolonized *sitio y lengua*. Our challenge now is to move beyond ourselves to seek further relevance of our work and of our positions within universities.

Notes

1. Albert Memmi, *The Colonizer and the Colonized* (Boston: Beacon Press, 1965).

2. Emma Pérez, "Notes from a Chicana Survivor," in Carla Trujillo (ed.), *Chicana Lesbians: The Girls Our Mothers Warned Us About* (Berkeley: Third Woman Press, 1991), pp. 159–184.

3. For example, we entitled the proceedings of the 1983 annual conference of the National Association for Chicano Studies (NACS) *Chicana Voices: Intersections of Class, Race, and Gender,* edited by Teresa Cordova *et al.* (originally published in 1986 and republished by Albuquerque: University of New Mexico Press, 1991). The title reflected the conversations of the day among Chicanas. As early as 1971, Chicanas were also using the concept "triple oppression." See, for example, Velia G. Hancock, "La Chicana: Chicana Movement and Women's Liberation," *Chicano Studies Newsletter 1:1* (February–March, 1971) .

4. I refer to *re-colonization* to suggest that the impacts of economic restructuring create new structures of exploitation and domination in communities of color worldwide.

5. Teresa Córdova, "Roots and Resistance: The Emergent Writings of Twenty Years of Chicana Feminist Writings" in Felix Padilla (ed.), *Handbook of Hispanic Culture: Sociological Volume* (Houston: Arte Publico Press, 1994), pp. 175–202.

6. Arte Publico Press omitted five pages of citations from the original document, including many that were cited in the text. The missing 88 citations included the works of Lillian Castillo-Speed, Teresa Córdova, Marta Cotera, Marta Lopez-Garza, Cynthia Orozco, Mary Pardo, Emma Pérez, Beatríz Pesquera, Mary Helen Ponce, Estela Portillo-Trambley, Naomi Quiñonez, Alvina Quintana, Anita Quintanilla, Tey Diana Rebolledo, Bertha Romero, Mary Romero, Vicki Ruiz, Elba

Sanchez, Marta Sanchez, Rosaura Sanchez, Chela Sandoval, Denise Segura, Christine Sierra, Rosalía Solorzano, Shirlene Soto, Carmen Tafolla, Rosario Torres Raines, Carla Trujillo, Gina Valdéz, Melba Vasquez, Anna González, Angelina Veyna, Evangelina Vigil, Alma Villanueva, Helena María Viramontes, Yvonne Yarbro-Bajarano, Lea Ybarra, and Patricia Zavella. The *Handbooks* were expensive and not readily available. For a copy of "Roots and Resistance" or the omitted citations contact the author at the School of Architecture and Planning, University of New Mexico, Albuquerque, NM 87131, USA.

7. Córdova, *op. cit.*, 1994, p. 175.

8. See also Alma Garcia's recently edited volume *Chicana Feminist Thought: The Basic Historical Writings* (New York: Routledge Press, 1997).

9. Mujeres en Marcha, "Chicanas in the 80s: Unsettled Issues" (Berkeley: Chicano Studies Library Publication Unit, 1983).

10. Córdova *et al.* (eds), *op. cit.*, 1991.

11. The work of Ada Sosa Riddel, Professor of Political Science and Chicano Studies at the University of California Davis, has been critical to the formation and continuation of MALCS.

12. Chela Sandoval, "U.S. Third World Feminism: The Theory and Method of Oppositional Consciousness in the Postmodern World," *Genders* 10 (1991), pp. 1–24.

13. Córdova, "Foreword," in Córdova *et al.* (eds.), *op. cit.*, 1991.

14. *Perspectives in Mexican American Studies,* Vol. 5 (1995).

15. Yvonne Yarbro-Bejarano, "Chicana Literature from a Chicana Feminist Perspective" in María Herrera-Sobek and Helena María Viramontes (eds.), *Chicana Creativity and Criticism: New Frontiers in American LIterature* (Albuquerque: University of New Mexico Press, 1996), p. 215.

16. Alicia Gaspar de Alba, in Ray Gonzalez (ed.), *Without Discovery: A Native Response to Columbus* (Seattle: Broker Moon Press, 1992), pp. 91–112.

17. Ibid, p. 112.

18. Emma Pérez, *Gulf Dreams* (Berkeley, CA: Third Woman Press, 1996).

19. Naomi Quiñónez, "El Salvador," in Roberta Fernandez (ed.), *In Other Words: Literature by Latinas of the United States* (Houston: Arte Publico Press, 1994), p. 159.

20. Carmen Tafolla, "In Guatamala," in Roberta Fernandez, *ibid.*, p. 182.

21. Cherrie Moraga, from *Last Generation*, in Roberta Fernandez, *ibid.*, p. 302.

22. Demetria Martinez, from *Mother Tongue*, in Lillian Castillo-Speed (ed.), *Women's Voices from the Borderlands* (New York: Touchstone Books, 1995), p. 275.

23. Ana Castillo, *Massacre of the Dreamers: Essays on Xicanisma* (Albuquerque: University of New Mexico Press, 1994), p. 11.

24. Tey Diana Rebolledo, *Women Singing in the Snow* (Tucson: University of Arizona Press, 1995), pp. 49–81.

25. Gloria Anzaldúa, *Borderlands: The New Mestiza* (San Francisco: Aunt Lute Press, 1987).

26. Angie Chabram Dernersesian, "And, Yes . . . The Earth Did Part: On the Splitting of Chicana/o Subjectivity," in Pesquera and de la Torre (eds.), *Building with Our Hands* (Berkeley: University of California Press, 1993), pp. 34–56.

27. Alicia Gaspar de Alba, *Sor Juana's Second Dream*, forthcoming.

28. Lara Medina, "Los Espíritus Siguen Hablando: Chicana Spiritualities," in Carla Trujillo (ed.), *Living Chicana Theory* (Berkeley: Third Woman Press, 1997), pp. 189–213.

29. Angie Chabram Dernersesian, *op. cit.*, p. 42.

30. Rosa Linda Fregoso, "The Mother Motif in *La Bamba and Boulevard Nights*," in Pesquera and de la Torre (eds.), *op. cit.*, pp. 130–148. See also *The Bronze Screen: Chicana and Chicano Film Culture* (Minneapolis: University of Minnesota Press, 1993).

31. Marta Cotera, "Caballero and Its Gendered Critique of Nationalist Discourse," *Perspectives in Mexican American Studies*, Vol. 5 (1995), pp. 151–170.

32. Yvette Flores-Ortiz, "Voices from the Couch: The Co-Creation of a Chicana Psychology," in Carla Trujillo (ed.), *op. cit.*, pp. 102–122.

33. Yvette Flores-Ortiz, "La Mujer y La Violencia: A Culturally Based Model for the Understanding and Treatment of Domestic Violence in Chicana/Latina Communities," in Mujeres Activas en Letras y Cambio Social (eds.), *Chicana Critical Issues* (Berkeley: Third Woman Press, 1993), pp. 169–182.

34. *Ibid.*, p. 173.

35. Flores-Ortiz, *op. cit.*, 1997, p. 119.

36. Antonia Castañeda, "Sexual Violence in the Politics and Policies of Conquest: Amerindian Women and the Spanish Conquest of Alta California," in Pesquera and de la Torre (eds.), *op. cit.*, p. 29.

37. Antonia Castañeda, "Presidarias y Pobladoras: The Journey North and Life in Frontier California," in Mujeres Activas en Letras y Cambio Social (eds.), *op. cit.*, 1993, p. 75.

38. Deena Gonzalez, "La Tules of Image and Reality: Euro-American Attitudes and Legend Formation on a Spanish–Mexican Frontier," in Pesquera and de la Torre (eds.), *op. cit.*, pp. 75–90.

39. *Ibid.*, p. 80.

40. *Ibid.*, p. 87.

41. Mary Romero, *Maid in the U.S.A.* (New York: Routledge, 1992).

42. Elisa Facio, *Understanding Older Chicanas* (Thousand Oaks, CA: Sage Publications, 1996).

43. Pesquera, "In the Beginning He Wouldn't Lift Even a Spoon: The Division of Household Labor," in Pesquera and de la Torre (eds.), *op. cit.*, pp. 181–195.

44. de la Torre, "Hard Choices and Changing Roles among Mexican Migrant *Campesinas*," in Pesquera and de la Torre (eds.), *op. cit.*, pp. 168–180.

45. Marta Lopez Garza, forthcoming.

46. Pat Zavella, "The Politics of Race and Gender: Organizing Chicana Cannery Workers in Northern California" in Mujeres Activas en Letras y Cambio Social (eds.), *op. cit.*, pp. 127–155.

47. María Alaníz *et al.*, "Immigrants and Violence: The Importance of Neighborhood Context," *Hispanic Journal of Behavioral Sciences* 20:2 (1998), pp. 155–174. Also, María Alaniz *et al.*, "Reinterpreting Latino Culture in the Commodity Form: The Case of Alcohol Advertising in the Mexican American Community," *Hispanic Journal of Behavioral Sciences* 17:4 (1995), pp. 430–451.

48. Community based research is increasingly being used in fields of planning, education, and public health. For a discussion of how this

approach is relevant to Chicano and Chicana Studies, see Teresa Córdova, "Plugging the Brain Drain: Bringing our Education Back Home," forthcoming.

49. Juana Mora, "The Treatment of Alcohol Dependency among Latinas: A Cultural, Feminist and Community Perspective," *Alcohol Treatment Quarterly* 16:1/2 (1998); "The Treatment of Alcohol Dependency Among Latinas: A Cultural, Feminist, and Community Perspective," in M. Delgado (ed.), *Alcohol Use/Abuse Among Latinos: Issues and Examples of Culturally Competent Services* (New York: Haworth Press, 1998); and "Learning to Drink: Early Drinking Experiences of Chicana/Mexicana Women," *Voces: A Journal of Chicana/Latina Research* 1:1 (1997), pp. 89–111.

50. For comprehensive citations of works on Chicana social movement activists, labor organizers, and workers, see Teresa Córdova, "Grassroots Mobilizations by Chicanas in the Environmental and Economic Justice Movement," *Voces: A Journal of Chicana/Latina Studies* 1:1 (1997a), pp. 31–55.

51. Cynthia Orozco, "Beyond Machismo, La Familia, and Ladies Auxiliaries: A Historiography of Mexican–Origian Women's Participation in Voluntary Association and Politics in the United States, 1870–1990," *Perspectives in Mexican American Studies,* 5 (1995), pp. 1–34.

52. See Elizabeth Martínez, "'Chingón Politics' Die Hard: Reflections on the First Chicana Activist Reunion," in Carla Trujillo, *op. cit.,* 1997, pp. 123–135. See also Alma Garcia, *op. cit.,* 1997.

53. Teresa Córdova, *op. cit.,* 1997a.

54. *Ibid.,* p. 49.

55. For example, Jeanne Gauna, Co-Director of the Southwest Organizing Project, writes regularly in *Voces,* the organization's newsletter; Elizabeth "Betita" Martinez writes for *Z Magazine;* and Patrisia Gonzalez, a syndicated columnist, writes regularly with her husband Roberto Rodriguez in their *Column of the Americas.*

56. Emma Pérez, "Notes from a Chicana Survivor," in Trujillo (ed.), *op. cit.,* 1991, pp. 159–184. Another version of this paper was published as "Speaking from the Margin: Uninvited Discourse on Sexuality and Power," in Pesquera and de la Torre, *op. cit.,* pp. 57–74.

57. *Ibid.,* p. 169.

58. *Ibid.*, p. 162.

59. *Ibid.*, p. 171.

60. *Ibid.*, p. 172.

61. *Ibid.*, p. 172.

62. *Ibid.*, p. 173.

63. *Ibid.*, p. 173.

64. *Ibid.*, p. 161.

65. Sandoval, *op. cit.*, p. 11.

66. Emma Pérez, "Irigaray's Female Symbolic in the Making of Chicana Lesbian Sitios y Lenguas (Sites and Discourse)," in Trujillo (ed.), *op. cit.*, 1997, pp. 87–101.

67. *Ibid.*, p. 88.

68. Teresa Córdova, "Power and Knowledge: Colonialism in the Academy," in Trujillo (ed.), *op. cit.*, 1997, pp. 17–45.

69. *Ibid.*, p. 41.

70. Deena González, "Speaking Secrets: Living Chicana Theory," in Trujillo (ed.), *op. cit.*, 1997, pp. 46–77.

71. *Ibid.*, p. 69.

72. Córdova, *op. cit.*, 1997b.

Luis Aponte-Parés
University of Massachusetts, Boston

Lessons from *el Barrio*—The East Harlem Real Great Society/Urban Planning Studio: A Puerto Rican Chapter in the Fight for Urban Self-Determination*

Abstract *During the 1960s, the Lower East Side and East Harlem were among the principal contested terrains in New York City, and the emerging Puerto Rican community was being challenged on many fronts. As contested terrains, they were the arenas where transforming forces in American society were being articulated. Responses to these forces varied from neighborhood to neighborhood. Among the responses were groups organized around community development, particularly to fight urban renewal projects. In this essay, I examine a year in the life of the East Harlem Real Great Society/Urban Planning Studio (RGS/UPS). RGS/UPS emerged in a transition period in the development of Puerto Rican institutions. It combined several characteristics of groups organized during those years. It was founded by grassroots community youth; it was also a professionally staffed organization; it was structured around an advocacy model; and it valued its ethnic-specificity, its Puertoricanness. Its staff's eagerness to speak for the needs and aspirations of Puerto Ricans was a clear example of ethnicity-based struggle.*

During the 1960s, the Lower East Side and East Harlem were among the principal *contested terrains* in New York City, and the emerging Puerto Rican community was being challenged on many fronts. Both neighborhoods had become key "homelands" to the Puerto Rican community as well as the theaters where much of their history had been recorded. As *contested terrains*, they were the arenas where transforming forces in American society, the economic, urban, and cultural spheres,

0739–3148/98/040399–22 © 1998 Caucus for a New Political Science

were being articulated during the period. Responses to these forces varied from neighborhood to neighborhood. Among the responses were groups organized around community development, particularly to fight urban renewal projects. One such group that had emerged in 1964 in the Lower East Side, *Loisaida*, and had expanded north to East Harlem, el Barrio, by 1967 was the Real Great Society.

In this essay, I examine a year (1969–1970) in the life of the East Harlem Real Great Society/Urban Planning Studio (RGS/UPS). In 1969 RGS/UPS completed assembling its professional team with people recruited from NYC, several other US cities, as well as Puerto Rico. During that year the organization was involved in key issues and key institutions that would shape East Harlem for years. I also review the organization's goals and strategies. Finally, I comment on some of the events that led to the demise of the organization which also took place that year.

I set the development of RGS/UPS within the Puerto Rican community's institutional history, and the *politics of place*, the struggle Puerto Ricans became involved in to resist their total displacement from key districts in the city. I also frame the analysis within the discourse of advocacy architecture/planning, a paradigm that challenged the underlying premises of traditional planning and was at the core of RGS/UPS tenets.

From Bodegas to Urban Renewal

From Colonia to Community by Virginia Sánchez-Korrol tells the story of Puerto Ricans in New York City.[1] Thus, the story of Puerto Ricans in NYC follows the story of the young city early in its development through its industrial (1850s–1920s) and corporate (1920s–present) stages. During each period there were push–pull factors which triggered the migration of different sectors of Puerto Rican society. During each migratory period Puerto Ricans created cultural, political, social, and/or action/advocacy organizations reflecting the complex composition of the community, i.e. class, political orientation, geography, gender, etc., as well as the severity of the challenge posed to them by problems emerging during each period. Settlement patterns differed responding to local conditions, employment opportunities, history of the neighborhood, and the quality of the neighborhood's support systems and institutional infrastructure.

Antonia Pantoja specifies three post-WWII eras in institution building in the Puerto Rican community. *The First Era (1945–1960)* is the end of the Hispanic organizing period and the early stages of Puerto Rican-centered organizing, a period during which "we called ourselves Puerto Ricans, and effectively challenged and replaced the non-Puerto Rican leadership who had elected themselves spokes people for Puerto Ricans in the larger society."[2] During this same period Puerto Ricans began to "form community consciousness" and began "representing" themselves on the built environment in earnest. Through the deliberate naming, decoration, and signage of bodegas, social clubs, political clubs, and restaurants, for example, Puerto Ricans, like other ethnic groups before them, began reshaping and appropriating the otherwise ordinary industrial city landscapes by building and claiming enclaves that looked like them, what Lefebvre calls *representational spaces*.[3] Thus, *las colonias* were the essential building blocks for the development of the community: the places where they could build identity in the urban milieu; the places where people made primary "life spaces," i.e. the areas people occupied in which their "dreams were made, and their lives unfolded"[4] and where historical events could be recorded and then remembered.

Pantoja associates the *Second Era (1960–1974)* with the Civil Rights Movement, Black Power, the War in Vietnam, etc., and identifies it as one of "growth and stabilization."[5] It was during the early part of this period (1955–1965) that settlement patterns changed from *colonias* into *barrios* or neighborhood enclaves, where Puerto Ricans continued to "build community" by shaping further the many small enclaves of earlier periods. However, this "growth and stabilization" was marred by the onslaught of these enclaves by the restructuring forces of the period. While Puerto Ricans were knitting a community in the *ghetto*, slum clearance and urban renewal were unweaving the work of a generation: the *deterritorialization* of a whole community. This period was marked by the emergence of professionally staffed service institutions and institutionalized movements for advocacy.[6] Key to this period, furthermore, was the awakening of *Nuyoricanness,* and with it the airing of the "unspoken grievance that Puerto Rican New Yorkers held against the island Puerto Rican elite."[7] In addition, the "young turks," as Pantoja calls them, were represented by youth that had become immersed in the Civil Rights Movement and in the movement for the independence of Puerto Rico framed by third-world revolutionary struggles.

Anti-poverty programs that emerged during this period had a profound effect on the character of Puerto Rican organizations. While providing funds for needed social services, they also fostered the bureaucratization of these institutions. The end result was that "voluntary work was replaced by paid work."[8] José Sánchez is less charitable about those who took over the struggle: "They usurped for themselves an empty language of resistance as well as the very real pain of Puerto Rican suffering in the interest of funding proposals and service delivery quotas."[9] Sánchez further argues that with the establishment of key agencies during the 1950s and '60s the stage was set for the "instrumentalist and therapeutic approach to community development that proved significant to Puerto Rican community history."[10] The *Third Era (1975 to the present)* is characterized by Pantoja as one of great advancement.[11]

Intersections and Transformations: The Politics of Place and Identity

Since the founding of the earliest of *colonias,* Puerto Rican settlement has been a struggle between opposing economic, social, cultural, and political forces. The will to settle and shape a community has been tempered by forces against these attempts. Underlying these forces are the contradictions between what Lefebvre calls "abstract space that arises from economic and political practices, and social space that arises from the use values produced by the residents in their pursuits of everyday life."[12]

As early as the 1920s, settlement in New York City by Puerto Ricans was marred with the politics of place: who controlled the underlying structure supporting the community, i.e. the housing, the stores, the street corners—the places of everyday life.[13] When Puerto Ricans were moving to New York City in great numbers during the early postwar period, there were momentous transformations taking place in the city. The emerging post-industrial city had no need for housing structures built for industrial workers of earlier periods: Puerto Ricans lived in neighborhoods where a large number of these buildings were deemed to be surplus. A poor community like them generally lacked the institutional infrastructure or framework to devise strategies to stop their displacement.

Until the late 1950s the majority of Puerto Ricans lived in Manhattan close to manufacturing jobs, and in neighborhoods that had been previously home to other ethnic groups then moving to suburbia. In fact, in the 1930s more than 75% of Puerto Ricans lived in Manhattan, their numbers dropping slowly throughout the 1950s to 60% and finally less than 50% by 1960. This was the period when the federal government engaged in full in the project of restructuring cities, and the beginning of *displacement and dispersal period* for the Puerto Rican community in New York City. It was during this period when what had been the early stage of *ethnic enclaves,* with some semblance of community with a myriad of "life spaces," became redundant. Residents of these neighborhoods were being pushed to the "outer boroughs," to the "neverland" of the "projects" in places like Far Rockaway, the South Bronx, etc. The move to the Bronx and Brooklyn in many cases provided cause for celebration since Puerto Ricans were moving to better quality housing than the older slums of Manhattan; however, as Sánchez puts it, "these moves also helped to undermine a major source of their survival as workers—their kinship ties."[14]

Between 1960 and 1990, while there was a net increase of Puerto Ricans in New York City, there was a loss of 70,661 Puerto Ricans living in Manhattan. *More than half of the loss occurred between 1960 and 1970, when 40,316 Puerto Ricans left*

the borough, the largest loss in the last three decades. The loss
between 1970 and 1980 was close to half the previous decade,
and between 1980 and 1990, again half as many moved away
from Manhattan. It should be noted that during the 1970s there
was reversed migration to Puerto Rico. Furthermore, dispersal
to other boroughs like Queens, the Bronx, and Brooklyn may
account for some of those who left Manhattan, signaling a residential divergence and economic stratification of the Puerto
Rican community. However, it could be argued that the bulk of
the loss was due to the displacement produced by the loss of
affordable housing units in Manhattan and the inability of
Puerto Ricans to gain full access to public housing and other
subsidized projects.[15] *It should also be noted that, even though
Manhattan gained population between 1980 and 1990 and a significant number of Dominicans and Mexicans moved to Northern
Manhattan, the loss of Puerto Rican and Latino populations in
Manhattan has continued.*

Location of the Struggle: Contested Territory
By the 1960s East Harlem and the Lower East Side had become
two major "homelands" for Puerto Ricans in the US. Although
both neighborhoods were in Manhattan and there were other
Puerto Rican neighborhoods in Brooklyn (like Red Hook) that
were as old, East Harlem and the Lower East Side had gained
symbolic significance and were considered by many the "centers" of Puerto Rican culture in the city. Both neighborhoods
represented two sides of the postwar spatial restructuring of
New York City in housing—that is, a decline in the needs of traditional industrial workers' residential districts (East Harlem)
and the reconfiguring of the traditional slum to attract the new
"baby boom" generation (Lower East Side). In East Harlem it
took the form of massive disinvestment by the abandonment of
major housing tracts, with selective redevelopment through
government-sponsored housing (public housing projects and
middle-income enclaves). The Lower East Side, although experiencing similar restructuring earlier, remained more attractive
for reinvestment due to its location between downtown and

midtown. In geographical terms, East Harlem became part of the *lumpengeography of capital,*[16] while the Lower East Side experienced gentrification articulated by a "frontier motif," i.e. neighborhoods where "hostile landscapes are regenerated, cleansed, reinfused with middle-class sensibility" and where the new "settlers," brave pioneers, go "where no (white) man has gone before."[17]

El Barrio
> La calle 116 es una calle puertorriqueña. ¡Vivimos alli tantos y tantos! Se oye a veces más español que inglés. Pase usted por la calle, y nada de extraño tiene que oiga una danza de Puerto Rico.[18]

East Harlem has been home to almost all ethnic groups that had succeeded each other from the late 19th century through the 1940s. Beginning in the 1930s and through the 1960s Greater Harlem, the "homeland" for New York City's African Americans, was re-articulated to include Puerto Ricans in "Spanish Harlem," or *el Barrio Latino.* By the 1950s, 116th Street became a Puerto Rican shopping district with an agglomeration of bodegas, *cuchifritos,* record and music shops, bakeries, travel agencies, and a whole assortment of other urban amenities to be found in any urban neighborhood. *La Marqueta,* which spanned between 111th and 116th Streets on Park Avenue, was a Puerto Rican shopper's Mecca. La 116 was also home to *El Ponce de León* and *San Juan,* the closest to Puerto Rican white-tablecloth restaurants in Manhattan.

However, by the 1960s East Harlem was *contested terrain,* between Puerto Ricans and African Americans to the north, east, and west, and between Puerto Ricans and powerful development forces south of 106th Street, particularly the 96th Street corridor, the traditional "DMZ Zone" between East Harlem and Yorkville, a working-class Irish neighborhood. By 1969 much of the history of Puerto Ricans in *el Barrio,* and *Loisaida* as well as other parts of Manhattan and Brooklyn had been erased. East Harlem's built environment had been mutilated by countless slum clearance projects that crisscrossed from east to west and north to south. *Los Proyectos* were the few places at the time where African Americans and Puerto Ricans shared common ground. East Harlem also had middle-income cooperative enclaves, and in general most Puerto Ricans could not afford to pay the cost of buying them, even though they were choice projects with moderate prices. Thus, African Americans were tenant majorities in the middle-income enclaves.

It has been argued that the purpose of urban renewal centered on complementary strategies for achieving two closely related ends: to buffer city centers and their commercial and cultural institutions from the tide of African American and Puerto Rican migration, and at the same time to reinforce territorial segregation through zoning and carefully coordinated location of schools, etc.[19] The eventual result of urban renewal was the destruction of four units of low-income housing for each one built, with a net decrease of low-income housing stock of 90% during the 1950s.[20] In some neighborhoods it entailed a fight between two groups attempting to retain the limited control they could have over their environment: who would do the development and who would move to it once the project was finished. Given the relatively weaker institutional base of Puerto Ricans in New York City, as compared to African Americans,[21] Jews, and whites in general, the fight was usually lost by Puerto Ricans, particularly in Manhattan.

By the late 1960s and early 1970s, land in East Harlem, as well as other similar neighborhoods throughout New York City, was "deeded" to a number of housing *caciques,* who in turn ruled small fiefdoms. By 1969, there had been an impasse around the issue of land development between African Americans and Puerto Ricans, and a truce had been "signed" between them, particularly between the Central Harlem and East Harlem politicos.[22] This truce implied the understanding that "you don't get in my turf, and I don't get into yours." The displacement of Puerto Ricans from Manhattan had accelerated during the 1960s (Table 1), and East Harlem's Puerto Rican population was at risk of new and massive displacement. In the midst of these territorial fights, RGS/East Harlem comes into the picture.

Table 1. Puerto Rican displacement from Manhattan: 1930–1990

Borough	1930	1940	1950	1960	1970	1980	1990
Manhattan	34,715	54,000	138,507	225,639	185,323	166,328	154,978
Gain/loss		+29,315	+133,107	+87,132	–40,316	–18,995	–11,300

Source: Census

The Real Great Society: The East Harlem Branch

The Real Great Society (RGS) was founded in the Lower East Side of Manhattan in 1964 by former gang leaders who teamed up to "fight poverty instead of each other."[23] The East Harlem branch (RGS/UPS) was organized in 1967 also by former gang leaders who along with young professionals wanted to be "at the center of the struggle for total environmental control."[24] RGS was founded during Pantoja's *Second Period* marked by professionally staffed organizations and by "young turks."

In three short years RGS became three different organizations. One was made up of the original founders which included former gang members and white "visionaries." The founders' group lost control of RGS around 1968 after a protracted struggle between those who wanted an organization open to all persons regardless of racial or national origin (RGS), and those supporting the view that Puerto Ricans had to make it on their own (RGS/UPS). The second organization, which emerged around 1967, was centered around the University of the Streets project, a concoction closer to the "typical" anti-poverty agency that emerged during the period, controlled at the beginning by the original group, but which had, in fact, turned into an African American and white organization.[25] The third was the East Harlem branch established by Angelo (Papo) Giordani in 1967 on 1673 Madison Avenue at 111th Street that began a remedial education center for high school dropouts. Papo and a few of his East Harlem friends recruited two dozen dropouts, and several East Harlem college students volunteered as summer instructors. Papo then became RGS vice-president for East

Harlem. Thus, the enlarged inner-core group included a half-dozen more members in an uptown wing which came to be referred to as RGS/Uptown, or RGS/East Harlem.[26]

With the founding of RGS/Uptown, RGS entered its second phase into its development. This founding marked the end of the original scheme, and the emergence of a new vision. The East Harlem branch was started by youth who had grown up in the streets the same as the gang leaders on the Lower East Side. By adding skills from conventional society to the raw skills of survival learned in the streets, the uptown leaders developed a "potent brand of sophistication, and RGS/East Harlem took on a very different pattern of development from that which characterized the original wing of the organization."[27] As one observer put it, "the uptown group was much more intense, more deliberate, more hard line, and more structured. But in terms of method and style and purpose, it was far more revolutionary, more conscious of race and Puerto Rican nationalism, and much more attuned to the militancy of current minority revolt."[28]

Within weeks of its founding a three-day riot broke out in East Harlem. The riot was triggered by the killing of a young Boricua by a policeman, perceived by many East Harlem residents as another example of police brutality.[29] Angelo (Papo) Giordani and others in RGS/East Harlem went out to calm the riots but found that attempts to take a few kids out of the neighborhood to the suburbs or elsewhere for a cooling off period was met with resistance. In a final attempt to find relief, Angelo went to Columbia University. In August 1967, barely a month after the East Harlem riots, at the request of Angelo Giordani the Division of Urban Planning of Columbia University sponsored a two-day conference called "The First East Harlem Youth Conference."[30] RGS/East Harlem co-sponsored the event and Angelo Giordani chaired the conference. Scores of teens were brought to Columbia to attend the conference, and the University provided room and board in its dormitories for them.

The list of dignitaries and important invitees included the Chief Executives of Metropolitan Life and Equitable Life

Insurance companies. Also included were high ranking officials of several banks, faculty members from Columbia, as well as Columbia scholars/dignitaries like Hank Bell and Charles Abrams. Willie Vázquez recalls the conference as "one that a who's who in New York City came to. Además de los blancos riquitos, there were people like Pedro Pietri and Piñero. It was very cool. Although the first day they tried to control the conference we were able to set the agenda, and by the second day we were in charge."

The result of the conference was a new and rebuilt image for RGS, one that would shift the power within the organization to the uptown branch. Two organizations were re-energized as a result of the conference: Young Citizens for Progress, headed by Angelo Giordani, and the East Harlem College Society, headed by Micky Meléndez.[31] Young citizens brought together high school dropouts, while the College Society was a mentoring and tutoring program to help young people to obtain a college education, who would then return to the neighborhood and apply their talents to its improvements. The effect of establishing these two organizations was that during a very short period (1967–1969), some of the "sharpest young people" in East Harlem joined forces with the East Harlem wing of RGS.[32]

The idea to bring together the youth and their mentors together under a single umbrella followed. The East Harlem Education Center, a.k.a. the East Harlem Prep School, became the dream of Papo, Bruce Young Candelaria, and others.[33] Finding a suitable environment and a place of their own became necessary. The idea finally evolved into the RGS/Town House Project. Project requirements called for ample spaces to house an ambitious program, and RGS/East Harlem was able to identify two five-story tenements on 110th Street between Madison and Park Avenues.[34] The Prep School became the place where "things were happening." As Young-Candelaria puts it:

> I remember that painting the Puerto Rican flag on the storefront made residents focus on our activities. They would come in and browse, and finally join the

rest of us. The most important thing that happened was that community residents began to flow naturally to the prep school, thus providing RGS with a real direct connection to the neighborhood and the community, while providing residents of the area with an alternative space, a "genuine" community-controlled institution. We started teaching GED, art classes, Spanish, English, and an array of other skills we never dreamt before opening the school.

The other major result of the conference was the establishment of a planning studio. During 1968 the School of Architecture at Columbia brought together a group of students, a studio professor, and RGS/Uptown. Under the leadership of Willie Vázquez, the studio engaged in a year-long study of projects in East Harlem. However, the results of its operation were mixed. The studio had been envisioned as a joint effort, an "experiment" bringing together the technical knowledge of architecture and planning students at Columbia, and the know-how and community knowledge of RGS, "to encourage architectural students to work with the realistic physical environmental problems of the community."[35] It was a difficult and uneasy partnership. Willie Vázquez recalls, "Eran unos blancos con ideas progresistas. Pero no querían oir nuestras opiniones. Ellos querían experimentar y no les gustaba que nosotros cuestionaremos sus ideas. It was during this time that Harry Quintana comes into the scene, and he really had a fit. He felt that the Columbia kids would not stay long enough for any of the projects to come through, thus leaving the community hanging."

It was the view that empowerment required that those in charge of development had to have a vested interest in it that drove RGS/Uptown in establishing the RGS/Urban Planning Studio as a follow up to the East Harlem Studio from Columbia University. In a 1969 funding proposal submitted to the Ford and Astor Foundations, RGS stated that, "The result of those two projects was the realization by the Real Great Society that East Harlem needed an architectural and planning resource

completely controlled by the community. As long as the technical resources necessary for physical development were controlled by forces outside the community," it was reasoned, "the
development itself would not be completely for the community."[36] By the summer of 1968 Harry Quintana, Willie Vázquez,
Angelo Giordani, Victor Feliciano, and others embarked into
the second phase of the RGS/East Harlem branch and founded
the Urban Planning Studio.

The Urban Planning Studio: 1968–1970

In 1968 Harry Quintana went to Yale University to complete his
architectural education. Quintana had been close to Columbia
University's East Harlem Planning Studio directed by Willie
Vázquez, but believed that in the end the "white kids" were going
to tire and leave behind unfinished projects.[37] Although some of
the young architects like Richard Rinzler and Bruce Dale
remained in RGS and were essential in the early development of
RGS/UPS during that same year, Harry decided to build a new
team that would provide the leadership in East Harlem. He
recruited some of the most vocal and committed young professionals in *el Barrio* and elsewhere in NYC in the areas of health,
education, and community planning. Assembling the team also
took him to Puerto Rico and Washington, DC, in 1969.

In Puerto Rico, Harry recruited three women: Carmen
Gloria Baba, Myrta Cruz, and Iris Concepción, who were fin-
ishing their graduate degrees in planning at the University of
Puerto Rico and were considering continuing their studies, pos-
sibly toward a PhD.[38] Getting architects took Harry to Princeton
and Washington, DC. At Princeton he recruited Mauricio
Gastón, a young architecture student. In Washington he went to
Catholic University where he met three Puerto Rican architec-
ture students from the School of Architecture at Catholic
University. They had been involved in radical politics at
Catholic University, in particular in the School of Architecture.
Like elsewhere in architecture schools throughout the nation
they had spent the best part of a year and a half in a fight against
the school's conservative faculty on issues centered around the

role of the architect in the inner city. Jaime Suárez, Luis Aponte-Parés, and Manuel (Neco) Otero accepted the offer to join RGS/UPS and in early June of 1969 arrived in East Harlem. There, they met another group of professionals, whites, Latinos, and African Americans that were being assembled by Harry, Willie, and Angelo: the team was completed.

Ideology: Advocacy and Self-Determination
Two visions guided the founding of RGS/UPS: a critical view of the architecture and planning professions, and the goal of community self-determination.

> Advocacy planning for the poor, if it is to have any real meaning, must be planning for power, planning for political and social change. It must serve to organize the community, help the community perceive and understand the working of the system by which it is oppressed, and direct political energies toward the realization of long range, as well as tangible short-range, goals, and these goals must be substantive—a larger share of the pie, different kinds and sizes of pies, the acquisition of real political power.[39]

> East Harlem is an underdeveloped country. Most of it is owned and controlled by private and governmental interests outside the community. In the past, the development of East Harlem has served these outside interests at the expense of an essentially powerless community, but this will not continue to be so. East Harlem is awakening to its rights and abilities for self control and self determination, and the balance of power has begun to shift towards the people. The people have become aware, as part of a nationwide movement, that they must control their own environment in order to determine their own future, and that control begins at the planning level through the utilization of the community's own environmentalists.[40]

During the 1960s there had been an ongoing debate among liberals on the merits of advocacy planning and citizen participation. Like Chester Hartman, cited above, Paul Davidoff had been a principal proponent of advocacy planning, which would openly invite political and social values to be examined and debated within the profession. This position was a clear rejection of planning prescriptions which had placed the planner as a "technician." In the 1950s under the rubric of "objective science," the planning profession had rejected any subjective role for planning and had promulgated the view that it was the planner's role to understand the functional aspects of the city and recommend appropriate future action to improve the urban condition. Davidoff argued that appropriate planning action could not be prescribed from a position of value neutrality, "for prescriptions are based on desired objectives."[41] Thus, planners had to go beyond explaining their values underlying their prescriptions: "he should affirm them. He should be an advocate for what he deems proper."[42]

Pluralistic planning, Davidoff argued, would provide a space where government planners, and the communities who were to be impacted by the proposed plans, would exchange views and negotiate alternatives. The problem was that those impacted the most were people of color, women, and the poor: the disenfranchised. Those who benefited from these actions were the real estate interests, construction industry, and the insurance and mortgage companies: the powerful. The advocacy of alternative plans by interest groups outside of government, Davidoff argued, would stimulate the debate in three ways: make the public more aware of the alternative choices offered; force the public agency to compete with other planning groups; and force those who have been critical of "establishment" plans to produce superior plans.[43] Where pluralistic planning principles were practiced, advocacy became the means of professional support for competing claims about how the community should develop.[44]

Advocacy planning had many supporters as well as detractors. One major detractor was Frances Fox Piven, who had argued that, although there was a tendency to "see professional advocates as free agents" and "ignore the federal dollars which support them and the federal interests they serve,"[45] they were fundamentally meeting the political needs of the Democratic Party in adjusting to population changes in the cities (mostly the migration of blacks from the south). In fact, these programs provided a battery of services not unlike those of old time political clubs. Planners, argued Piven, offered no concrete service or benefit. They offered their skill in the planning process, whose object, advocates said, was to overcome the "vast discrepancy in technical capacity between local communities and city bureaucracies."[46]

Piven had also argued that another implied message was the notion that "the urban poor can influence the decisions once they are given the technical help of a planner—or better still, once they actually learn the technical skills of planning."[47] Cooper Square in the Lower East Side, for example, had taken 10 years to develop an alternate plan. Their chief accomplishment, according to Piven, was to stop the early threat of urban renewal. Walter Thabit, one of the planners involved in the struggle, commented, "Protest without planning could have done as much."[48] Finally, Piven argued that involving local groups in "elaborate planning procedures is to guide them into a narrowly circumscribed form of political action, and precisely that form for which they are least equipped."[49] Advocate planners were "coaxing ghetto leaders off the streets," where they could make trouble.[50]

The advocacy that RGS/UPS was espousing differed from Davidoff's and Piven's views. In fact, Harry and others in RGS/UPS saw how Columbia's advocacy planning studio had failed. Their principal argument, while echoing Piven's, was that even *los blanquitos liberales* would never cross the line and attempt to disrupt the system, particularly since RGS/UPS saw itself as part of "oppositional movements." Between 1968 and 1970 RGS/UPS instigated protests by joining others in the community in civil disobedience: by burning trash on the streets and blocking traffic on the 125th Street entrance to the

Triborough Bridge.[51] As one observer noted, "In July 1968, when they felt the city was putting less antipoverty money into East Harlem than the area deserved, they decided to organize a demonstration. Every day for three days in accordance with a carefully worked-out strategy, youths holding hands, singing, and shouting formed human barricades across busy intersections at peak rush hours in First, Third, and Fifth avenues and created massive traffic jams.... Then all of a sudden a million more dollars came from Lindsay's office for summer jobs in East Harlem."[52]

Those at RGS/UPS expounded the view, furthermore, that the "problem" dwelt with "white professionals" and that self-determination through ethnic-centered development was good. Although the two views were not necessarily incompatible, RGS/UPS was partially basing their rhetoric in the long tradition of Puerto Rican radical politics in the US.[53] This view led Harry Quintana, Mauricio Gastón, and others in RGS/UPS to "invite" the Young Lords to join with RGS/UPS in a dual strategy: the Young Lords would raise the volume of protest and the political consciousness of community residents, energizing them by pointing toward the injustices of displacement, deficient health service, loss of jobs, etc., while RGS/UPS would "interpret" the options available for development and pursue those avenues with the most advantage for the community. Harry and others at RGS/UPS recognized that only through a massive grassroots response by the community residents to the nefarious policies being implemented through urban renewal would the power brokers, both in the neighborhood as well as the "white establishment," make adjustments and stop the displacement. However, the "arrangement" between RGS/UPS and the Young Lords did not bear fruit.[54]

RGS/UPS exhibited the contradictions raised by Piven while attaching itself to Davidoff's view that by developing alternate plans and bringing them to the "public forum" community residents had to benefit ultimately. In the absence of strong neighborhood-specific institutions, however, RGS/UPS reached for too many goals and played too many roles. Perhaps reviewing the organization's strategies and some projects will illustrate these tensions and contradictions.

Organization

The overall general plan of the UPS was to develop a strategy of resistance to displacement while affirming Puerto Ricans' right to be part of the urban culture. To this general strategy was added the dictum that only through a community effort could some of the problems affecting the Puerto Rican community then be solved. This strategy was articulated five ways in a proposal:

> To involve people of East Harlem in the physical development of their own community by assisting any East Harlem resident, group, or coalition to carry out realistic plans for the physical development of their community; to serve as advocate for East Harlem relative to any projects or programs which have been conceived or planned by interests outside the community; to initiate projects and programs which serve the community's interest; to use technical creativity to evolve new approaches to the problems of the physical environment; and to help increase the number of indigenous architects and planners in East Harlem by preparing local youths for careers in environment development by running employment and training programs.[55]

Operationally, RGS/UPS was organized in teams. Each team would usually be comprised of an architect, an urban planner, a lawyer, a community organizer, and a specialist in an area specific to the project. Each team could be involved in one or more projects. However since most in the staff were full time students at Columbia University and elsewhere, the load was extremely heavy. When one examines the array of projects that RGS/UPS was involved with between 1968 and 1970, it is clear that an attempt was made to address the five goals the organization had set itself to reach. By 1969 RGS/UPS had been involved in a number of projects: the development of five vest-pocket parks; Afro-Latin Unity Council Headquarters, a project of the Urban Coalition; the Town House and Prep School; a proposal on how to develop cooperative housing utilizing Old Law and New Law Tenements; facilities building for the East Harlem Triangle Urban Renewal Project; the Aguilar–Hellgate planning study; Barrio Nuevo Planning Study; and a counterproposal for 1199 cooperative housing. During the year two other projects were added: a consulting contract with the Board of Education for the development of an alternative to the Park East High School and the development of the health facilities and other facilities for the East Harlem Tenants Council's Taíno Towers Project.[56]

Projects[57]
During the 1960s the "edge" between East Harlem and Yorkville, a traditionally working-class white enclave, was always being challenged by real estate interests expanding the well-to-do Upper East Side further north by developing luxury and middle-class developments. Although there is a major land elevation change between the two communities, and just north of 96th Street, Metro North, the New Haven and other commuter railroads emerge from underground and become a large viaduct that divides East Harlem on Park Avenue, developers were looking at ways of entering the community. One way to reach this goal was to expand the Mt. Sinai Hospital north and east.[58] In the east, Metro North and East River urban renewal projects were "conquered" land, assuring staff at Metropolitan Hospital, doctors, nurses, and others, with moderate and middle-income housing in close proximity.

Barrio Nuevo was conceived by a group of local residents who wanted to hold the line from the expansion of Yorkville, Mt. Sinai, and Metro North. Under the leadership of a Colombian national, Edmundo Facini, a grassroots movement had been organized. Their area of "influence" was between 98th Street and 106 Street between Lexington and Third Avenue. This was also similar to the area delineated by HOPE community, a housing development group under the leadership of a white minister, Reverend Calvert. At the time Harry Quintana and others in RGS/UPS, as well as to Facini and others in the community, believed HOPE community's development schemes could easily merge with those interests from Yorkville, and thus a different plan had to be developed.[59] Two people were assigned to the project: Luis Aponte and Iris Concepción, an architect–urban designer and a social planner. During the year they went to meetings held in a storefront that had been configured into a theater environment by Facini and were usually very well attended. As part of the planning process all pertinent data were gathered, and all the real estate transactions taking place as landlords were assembling land for redevelopment identified. In addition, the redevelopment of a bus depot by the Transit Authority was looked at and evaluated. By the spring of 1970 development schemes had begun to be elaborated with the full support of community residents. The project taking shape was a model of participatory planning and promised to provide the neighborhood with an action plan that would guide its development to "mirror" the community's needs. However, while working on the preliminary material, in the early spring of 1970, Barrio Nuevo collapsed.[60]

The East Harlem Tenants Council (EHTC) had been a pioneering group in East Harlem, and their effort was centered around the redevelopment of two city blocks between 121st and 122nd Streets and between 1st and 2nd Avenues in East Harlem. Under the leadership of Ted Vélez, this project was one of the major sites in East Harlem where African Americans and Puerto Ricans came together and decided to work together toward a common goal. They had envisioned a very novel project which provided poor people with the urban comforts of the middle class. This project, which eventually was built as Taíno Towers, called for the development of a self-sustaining enclave that included housing, health services, an open air amphitheater, a gym with a swimming pool, space for a college, and plenty of commercial storefronts.

Some at RGS/UPS thought that the project as envisioned was too big, and that it would overwhelm the scale of the community, while displacing those living in the immediate neighborhoods.[61] During the year RGS/UPS staff began to address these concerns and began drafting an alternative proposal that would be less centralized and that could be more in context with the surrounding neighborhood, i.e. the tenements. RGS/UPS believed that, even though tenements were not the best building type for development, their scale was appropriate for the neighborhood. The experience of obliterating whole blocks of tenements and rebuilding them with "towers in the park" projects had not produced better neighborhoods and in fact had fractured the fabric of the community. The radical proposals expounded by RGS/UPS led to an unwillingness by the EHTC leadership to lend credibility to their work, or to listen to the ideas being presented.

The difficulties encountered, furthermore, were symptomatic of the period and in particular to East Harlem. If a group had "gained control" of a turf, the last thing they wanted to do was to challenge the way agencies worked. If these groups wanted to promote their "own vision," they had to do so in incremental ways, and in a language funding agencies understood and felt comfortable with. RGS/UPS nationalistic rhetoric, furthermore, threatened the compact between the group and the "establishment"; thus, no alternate proposal was ever developed. RGS's role was limited, therefore, to assistance in the development of a community-based health center.

The Park East High School project was centered around the development of a 4000-student high school to be built on the site of the old Rupert Brewery in the upper 90s in Manhattan. From the beginning both the East Harlem and Yorkville communities had challenged the project, but the Board of Education nevertheless hired a white firm, a society architect, for its design. RGS/UPS involvement came through the persona of Felicia Clark, an Upper East Side socialite, daughter of Senator Clark of Philadelphia, who was concerned about the size of the proposed high school, and felt that what East Harlem and the Upper East Side (Yorkville) needed was a more discreet and humane environment that would challenge students and provide real educational avenues linking students with the life of the city. RGS/UPS staff was involved developing an "alternative scheme" to the one the Board of Education was designing. The proposal called for the utilization of several small theme-centered schools that would open around the Rupert site, as well along Madison, Park, and Third avenues on a variety of places, including storefronts. On the Rupert site, the proposal called for a mixed-income housing project along with a much smaller school which included "anchor services" like a gymnasium, a theater, and other assorted community facilities that would be open to everyone, thus serving as resources to the community. The proposal also called for the adoption of each theme-centered school by a larger institution—i.e. the theater would be adopted by a Broadway and/or downtown producer, union, or artists, and students would learn their trade and skills by being part of the production of a drama or other work. The proposal was presented to the Park East High School Committee, the Board of Education, and the architect toward the spring of 1970. Although RGS/UPS was not involved in the eventual development of the project, the final result of the project was the development of Rupert Towers and a decentralized Park East Complex which looked very similar to the alternate scheme developed by Neco Otero, Jaime Suárez, and Luis Aponte-Parés.

Problems and Contradictions

When one examines these projects against the avowed strategies articulated by RGS/UPS in their proposal it is somewhat clear that a number of major challenges emerged. These challenges were brought about by both the realities of East Harlem and the specific way community development and housing took shape in the community.

The collapse of Pueblo Nuevo, the premier participatory planning project for RGS/UPS, signaled that even when the best of intentions were present other forces could take a toll. Generally, involving the community residents in a meaningful way, the fundamental tenet of RGS/UPS, became an insurmountable task. First, there were too many issues: housing, health, education, drugs, crime, etc.; and neighborhood residents were being asked to be superhuman. In any given weekday evening there were countless meetings around crime, housing, education, welfare, etc., and even those residents who wanted to get involved were stretched to their limits, most selecting wisely one or two areas with which to be involved. Furthermore, attempting to organize required resources and a clear strategy, both either missing or not well developed at RGS/UPS. The earlier association with the Young Lords proved to be unproductive, particularly when the Lords became entangled in nationalistic rhetoric and reached for citywide exposure. RGS/UPS remained focused on East Harlem and on the physical development of the community; thus the early connections lost their vitality.

Second, missing also in East Harlem were the appropriate neighborhood-specific forums and vehicles to organize the community, provide exposure, and debate ideas. The institutional infrastructure was either missing or very weak. Possibly the most important institution for community development during those years was the Community Planning Boards. These boards played only a minor role in development and appointees were many times suspect, due to conflict of interest. East Harlem residents, furthermore, had had their share of "community action programs," but these worked best when they were promoted by a strong local leadership, usually a clergyman, as in the African American community. The emerging leadership in the neighborhood differed greatly in their strategies. Those with political inclinations had clustered around organizing political clubs. Others had discovered opportunities in anti-poverty programs: they learned how to exploit poverty, becoming the notorious "poverty pimps" of the 1960s and 1970s. Some others learned to mix political clubs and anti-poverty programs, leading to the establishment of the Méndez and Del Toro political dynasties.

There were many others who were involved in other struggles in education reform, the development of health resources, housing advocacy, and joining the boards of community action agencies, etc. However, the "newness" of neighborhood-specific organizing required trials and errors, as the need to invent institutions demanded creativity, resources, and plenty of energy. Thus, although Puerto Ricans living in East Harlem were a community whose economic power had eroded, or never materialized, their chances for survival rested on individual actions, since those devising the strategies were overwhelmed, or did not choose grassroots organizing, nor envisioned a "movement" to deliver change.

Third, although both the "native" and outside staff at RGS/UPS were a majority of Puerto Ricans, all were very young, thus lacking in traditional authority in the eyes of the Puerto Rican/Latino community. The youth level, therefore, posed a real barrier for community residents to consider the "wisdom" of such "young turks" who were espousing radical thinking and calling for a revolt. The likelihood of developing such a following was next to zero.

Providing assistance to East Harlem residents to carry out plans was closer to the available organizational resources. By engaging in several projects the staff of RGS/UPS afforded some groups added resources and the ability to begin articulating their needs. Projects like Taíno Towers, Park East, and Aguilar–Hellgate drained most of the resources RGS/UPS had to offer, many times diminishing the potential effectiveness of the group's intervention in them. Possibly the most successful of all projects RGS/UPS worked on were the vest-pocket parks. The design of vest-pocket parks showed all of RGS/UPS's strength. These small parks were jointly selected by RGS/UPS and neighborhood residents in blocks where there was some community cohesion and where community input would be viable. Usually it entailed working with a youth organization of some kind, and involving block-specific youth in the design and final construction of the parks. This close collaboration guaranteed that the park would be "respected" by the local youth, i.e. no graffiti or vandalism. However, funding for the parks never included "maintenance" funds; thus, in many cases, these parks went into disrepair soon after, since the local neighborhood users lacked the material resources to repair them. Furthermore, many of these parks remained in an institutional limbo for many years since they did not belong to any particular city agency who would see for their long-term maintenance, etc.

Although the fundamental strategy of RGS/UPS was advocacy, serving as an advocate for all of East Harlem proved politically difficult. Groups in the housing struggle like the East Harlem Tenants Council, Concerned Citizens of East Harlem, the East Harlem Triangle, UPACA, and Metro North, for example, wanted their own voices heard and did not need RGS/UPS to speak for them. They had to "cut their own deals" with city authorities and thus had no use for or mistrusted the "intermediary" role of advocate planners. Furthermore, fundamental to RGS/UPS's vision was using "native" talent in the design of the local projects, particularly in the architecture and urban planning arenas, colliding with the vision of these groups, which like others in the city, selected their "talent" from either "name architects" or from "advocates" who were in direct competition for clients with RGS/UPS.[62] Furthermore, East Harlem had white, Puerto Rican, and black voices, and most of the time each wanted to speak for themselves. However, in at least one case RGS/UPS served the community well. By joining forces with African American architects and planners, Harry Quintana and others in RGS/UPS raised the issue of lack of representation of Latinos and African Americans in the City Planning Commission, a citywide body that had many of the key developmental powers, and whose decisions had long-term impact for all New Yorkers. In 1969 during an intensive lobbying period, RGS/UPS and ARCH, as well as elected officials and other leaders, joined hands by holding press conferences, mounting organized protests at the meetings of the American Institute of Architects, meeting with the Lindsay administration, and other professional forums. The result of this effort led to the appointment of an African American to the Commission.

Initiating projects and programs also proved difficult. The professional requirements necessary to develop proposals, etc., were many times beyond the technical capacities of the staff. On the fifth strategy, RGS/UPS was the most successful. Almost everyone attached to RGS/UPS through its two-year studio continued their careers in architecture, planning, or engineering, leading these professionals into further involvement with the community.

Demise

Beyond the contradictions exhibited within RGS that led to its ineffectiveness, the demise of RGS/UPS was brought about primarily by the untimely investigation by the Un-American Committee of the US Senate. It was widely believed at RGS/UPS that the event that triggered the McClellan Committee investigation was the support that RGS/UPS staff provided to the Young Lords during their take-over of the church on East Harlem. However, there had been other problems brewing, problems brought about by internal issues.

The struggle between the East Harlem and Lower East Side branches between 1968 and 1970 was debilitating and consumed too many hours of planning and strategizing, thus leaving less time for the task at hand. There had been other problems, including: class divisions, gender issues, ideological differences, homophobia, administrative disarray, and professional disparities among staff members.

The most noticeable problem dealt with class. Those who had been raised in Puerto Rico, particularly the staff that Harry had recruited from the island and Washington, had a very "middle-class" outlook and were seen by others in the staff as having attitudes of *blanquitos*. In fact, some *were blanquitos* and had chosen to work at RGS/UPS not fully understanding the class differences between those who came to the US for an education and those who grew up in a Puerto Rican *barrio*. Even though Harry Quintana and Angelo Giordani had been to even "better schools," i.e. Yale and Harvard, while those raised in Puerto Rico had been to "second tier" universities, their outlook differed significantly. For Harry and Papo and others at RGS/UPS, gaining access to a professional status was a culmination of their aspirations and a triumph. For those raised in Puerto Rico, including those who went to school on the island, going to college was within the expectations they grew up with. Except for economic barriers, none had grown up as a "minority" and thus did not have any sense of what it meant to be one at the time.[63] The second major area of problems was the gender issue, which was very closely associated with the class issue. Women in the staff had a discreet demeanor and expected some guarded language. The staff in general treated women with respect, but there was always an added sexual connotation and edge that were not well received by the women.

The ideological differences were more subtle. Some in the staff were avowed Marxists, while others were "liberals" who wanted to "join" the system for a better piece of the pie.[64] These ideological differences, furthermore, were also felt toward the issue of independence of Puerto Rico. To the surprise of some, many of those who grew up in New York wanted statehood for the island. This colored their view toward how to deal with the issues of language, culture, etc. Some of those in the staff from the island were *independentistas* who felt that such attitudes were close to "imperialist attitudes." Although no one in the staff was openly gay, at least two of the staff members were gay. This brought about a lot of discomfort, particularly when a staff member sent a young woman to "test" if one of them was a *maricón*. There was the usual homophobic comment day in and day out, and whenever there was someone visiting the office who was either an obvious or suspected gay or lesbian, including some community leaders, the staff made homophobic and bigoted remarks.

Finally, there was always a feeling that the administration of RGS/UPS was in a suspended reality. There was never any explanation of why things were done, and staff meetings were mostly left in limbo. There was an unevenness on the issue of work attendance and the completion of work, issues that were always difficult to deal with.

Conclusions

RGS and RGS/UPS were organized by Puerto Rican youth whose political awareness was being shaped by the cultural forces that had shaken the nation during the 1960s. With calls for "community empowerment," "advocacy planning," "citizen participation," etc., RGS/UPS espoused the language of those in the political arenas of the city, calling for a community's right in the development of their neighborhoods, a call requesting a "piece of the pie." As young Puerto Ricans, RGS and RGS/UPS founders were part of the oppositional forces which questioned the legitimacy of dominant cultural forces in American cities. As community organizers and activists, architects and planners, the staff of RGS/UPS developed a sophisticated understanding of the issues of the day.

This understanding served them well and enabled the organization to interject itself into the *contested terrains* in East Harlem. Thus, differently from the downtown branch, which remained outside the discourse and the central issues in the Lower East Side, i.e. educational reform and the housing struggle, RGS/UPS played a limited but important part in the central issues of East Harlem between 1968 and 1970. Indeed, I contend that even though RGS/UPS accomplished very few of its goals, its efforts challenged the legitimacy of the status quo in East Harlem by increasing the volume of protest, and for a while promoting what Mollenkopf calls a "new political space," where city politicos had to interact with a new set of actors vying for power. For a very short period, RGS/UPS attracted the attention of the power brokers in East Harlem by exposing the many contradictions inherent in the projects supported by local power brokers who had aligned themselves with the downtown politicos.

RGS/UPS emerged in a transition period in the development of Puerto Rican institutions. It combined several of the characteristics of groups organized during those years: it was founded by grassroots community youth; it was also a professionally staffed organization; it was structured around an advocacy model; and it valued its ethnic-specificity, its *Puertoricanness*. Its staff's eagerness to speak for the needs and aspirations of Puerto Ricans was a clear example of what Andrés Torres calls "ethnicity-based struggle." RGS/UPS also attempted to open a dialogue between white urban professionals (architects, urban designers, physical, social, and human services planners), Puerto Ricans, and other people of color.

Finally, RGS/UPS also emerged in a transition period in federal urban policy. By the late 1960s, protests arising from the fights against urban renewal gained the attention of federal authorities and a policy shift toward a more traditional urban policy took place. Model Cities, the last of the major programs directed at the urban crisis that HUD implemented, was channeled through city governments, the very political structures community action had been designed to bypass.[65] In the Puerto Rican community, some of these new organizations that had been established at the local neighborhood level revisioned Puerto Rican power and identity by appropriating the language of development, while searching for ways of articulating this identity and representing it in the urban landscape. Unfortunately, RGS/UPS emerged when the economic options for Puerto Ricans in New York City became significantly less promising, as they were becoming "surplus labor."

Notes

* I would like to thank former RGS/UPS staff that provided me with their insights and most of the historical background on the organization: Willie Vázquez, Harry Quintana, Victor Feliciano (founding members of RGS/UPS), RGS staff members Bruce Young Candelaria, Carmen Gloria Baba, Sara Myrta Cruz, and Jaime Suárez. I would also like to thank Bruce Dale who worked with the East Harlem Studio of Columbia University and with RGS/UPS as a consultant. This essay is built around the personal recollections of those actors contacted and those of the author. It is also based on two proposals submitted by RGS/UPS to the Ford Foundation and other foundations. In the proposals the philosophy of the organization is expounded and projects are discussed. The essay does not represent the opinions of those interviewed, nor is it the final work on RGS/UPS. I would also like to thank Professor Betty Woody of CPCS/U.MASS Boston for her critical suggestions on the manuscript.

1. Virginia Sánchez-Korrol, *From Colonia to Community: The History of Puerto Ricans in New York City from WWII to 1983* (Berkeley: University of California Press, 1994).

2. Antonia Pantoja, "Puerto Ricans in New York: A Historical and Community Development Perspective," *Centro* 11:5 (Spring 1989) (New York: Center for Puerto Rican Studies), p. 24.

3. Henri Lefebvre, translated by Donald Nicholson-Smith, *The Production of Space* (Cambridge: Blackwell Publishers, 1991), p. 33.

4. John Friedmann and Goetz Wolff, "World City Formation: An Agenda for Research and Action," *International Journal of Urban and Regional Research* 6:3 (1992), p. 326.

5. Pantoja, *op. cit.*, p. 25.

6. *Ibid.*, p. 24.

7. *Ibid.*

8. Carlos Rodríguez-Fraticelli and Amilcar Tirado, "Notes Towards a History of Puerto Rican Community Organizations in New York City," *Centro* IV:1 (1991), p. 42.

9. José Sánchez, *Housing Puerto Ricans in New York City, 1945 to 1984: A Study in Class Powerlessness*, PhD dissertation (New York: New York University, 1990), p. 339.

10. *Ibid.*, p. 327.

11. The Puerto Rican community's recent history is one of uneven development. In the next section we examine some of the barriers encountered by the community.

12. Lefebvre, *op. cit.*, p. 241.

13. Jesús Colón, "Un Puertorriqueño en Nueva York," in Juan Flores (ed.), *Divided Arrival. Narratives of the Puerto Rican Migration* (New York: Hunter College/Centro de Estudios Puertorriqueños, undated).

14. José Sánchez, *op. cit.*, p. 451.

15. *Ibid.*

16. Richard Walker, "Two Sources of Uneven Development Under Advanced Capitalism: Spatial Differentiation and Capital Mobility," *Review of Radical Political Economics* 10:3 (1978).

17. Neil Smith, "New City, New Frontier: The Lower East Side as Wild, Wild West," in Michael Sorkin (ed.), *Variations on a Theme Park: The*

New American City and the End of Public Space (New York: Noonday Press, 1992), p. 70.

18. Juan Huyke, "En Nueva York. Para Francisco Vizcarrondo," in Juan Flores (ed.), *Divided Arrival. Narratives of the Puerto Rican Migration* (New York: Centro de Estudios Puertorriqueños, Hunter College, 1984), p. 31.

19. Susan S. Fainstein and Norman I. Fainstein, "Neighborhood Enfranchisement and Urban Redevelopment," *Journal of Planning Education and Research* 2 (1982), pp. 67–81.

20. Scott A. Greer, *Urban Renewal and American Cities. The Dilemma of Democratic Intervention* (Indianapolis: Bobbs-Merrill, 1965), p. 56.

21. Andrés Torres, *Between Melting Pot and Mosaic: African Americans and Puerto Ricans in the New York Political Economy* (Philadelphia: Temple University Press, 1995).

22. The ongoing fight in East Harlem around the 125th Street commercial project, also known as the "Pathmark Site," is centered around an age old issue: who has the "right" to develop land in East Harlem? The two opposing groups represent on one side a coalition of some Puerto Ricans with an African American consortium and developer, the Abyssinian Church, and the East Harlem Triangle, the domain of Alice Kornegay, a long-time resident and developer of the northern end of East Harlem. This group is supported by Charles Rangel, the ranking African American in the US Congress, Guillermo Linares, the only elected official of Dominican descent, Frank Díaz, the former Assemblyman for East Harlem, and an assortment of white politicians like former Borough President Ruth Messinger. The other side gathers mostly Dominicans (National Supermarket Association, the owner of Bravo and Associated) and some Puerto Ricans, representing *bodegueros*, who are mostly Dominicans. The latter group is supported by Adam Clayton Powell IV. This fight is not new.

23. Roger Vaughan, "The Real Great Society," *Life Magazine* 63:11 (1967), p. 76.

24. Proposal submitted by RGS/UPS to the Ford and Astor Foundations, 1969, p. 4.

25. "Located as it was across the street from Tompkins Square Park, a hangout for the East Village hippie colony, the University of the Streets was virtually swamped by this transient middle-class population.

Probably eighty percent or more of the university's enrollment that summer was made up of young people who had come in from outside the neighborhood, largely from suburbia, searching for adventure and stimulation": Richard Poston, *The Gang and the Establishment* (New York: Harper and Row, 1971), pp. 77–78.

26. Interview with Willie Vázquez, July 1995.

27. Richard Poston, *op. cit.*, p. 106.

28. *Ibid.*

29. Willie Vázquez.

30. *Ibid.*

31. *Ibid.*

32. *Ibid.*

33. Interview with Bruce Young-Candelaria, summer 1996. Bruce had joined RGS as a Vista volunteer. During our interview he believed that what attracted him to RGS was the "fit" RGS had with the community.

34. The two lower floors were to be for institutional use, while the upper three floors were to have six two-bedroom and six three-bedroom apartments. The second story of the Town House was to be home to a library, classroom spaces, and individual and group areas. The ground floor was to have a meeting room, a recreation room, an art workshop, and a cafe. The cafe was to open to an adjacent empty lot which was to be developed into a "vest-pocket park." Vest-pocket parks became a common development alternative to the increasing empty lots produced by the disinvestment process going on in East Harlem. Although RGS/UPS was involved in the design and development of five vest-pocket parks with community participation, most went into disrepair within a short period of time.

35. RGS/UPS proposal, p. 7.

36. *Ibid.*, p. 6.

37. Interview with Harry Quintana, July 1995. His account differs from Bruce Dale's, who thought that the underlying problem was that the architecture students were not interested in planning projects and the East Harlem Studio was more of a planning than an urban design studio.

38. Of the three, Iris was the most comfortable with the idea. Having grown up in New York City, Iris was fluent in both Spanish and English, and her parents lived in Queens. Her father was a super in a building in Queens and had a good union job.

39. Chester Hartman, "The Advocate Planner: From 'Hired Gun' to Political Partisan," in Neil Gilbert and Harry Specht (eds.), *Planning for Social Welfare: Issues, Models, and Tasks* (New York: Prentice Hall, 1970), p. 59.

40. RGS/UPS proposal, p. 4.

41. Paul Davidoff, "The Advocate Relationship: Advocacy and Pluralism in Planning," in Gilbert and Specht, *op. cit.,* p. 192.

42. *Ibid.*

43. *Ibid.,* p. 195.

44. *Ibid.*

45. Frances Fox Piven, "Who Does the Advocate Planner Serve?" in Richard A. Cloward and Frances Fox Piven (eds.), *The Politics of Turmoil: Poverty, Race, and the Urban Crisis* (New York: Vintage Books, 1970), p. 44.

46. *Ibid.,* p. 45.

47. *Ibid.,* p. 46.

48. *Ibid.,* p. 47.

49. *Ibid.*

50. *Ibid.,* p. 48.

51. Interview with Harry Quintana.

52. Poston, *op. cit.,* pp. 108–109.

53. Having grown up in the Italian neighborhood of Pleasant Avenue in East Harlem, Harry remembers that the day after the Puerto Rican Nationalist Party attack on Blair House in Washington, DC, he tried to go to Franklin High and the "ginnies" were waiting to beat him up. In fact, the Italians would not permit him to go to school for a whole week (Quintana). Harry's interest on radical Puerto Rican politics was always linked to the Nationalist event.

54. In "The Young Lords Legacy: A Personal Account" (Crítica) Pablo Guzmán makes the connection between RGS/UPS and the Young Lords. In his rendition of the story, however, Guzmán does not specify that the organizing tool used by the Lords—i.e. getting brooms and sweeping the streets, and then burning the trash—had been previously utilized by RGS in 1968 and 1969. Willie Vázquez argues that when Guzmán, Luciano, and others came to East Harlem, they had lost connection to *el Barrio*, and that, in fact, had not Mauricio Gastón, Papo Giordani, and Harry Quintana urged them to get in contact with the Chicago Lords, etc., these "young Puerto Rican students would have never made the connections" (Vázquez). Due to space limitations we cannot fully explore the ideological issues that attracted and separated RGS/UPS and the Young Lords. A longer version of this essay will explore them.

55. RGS/UPS 1969 proposal, p. 28.

56. RGS/UPS proposal. During that same year the Architects Renewal Committee for Harlem was also developing an alternate plan for the State Office Building (SOB) being proposed for 125th Street. During the winter and early spring ARCH called RGS/UPS for help in the development of the project. A group of us spent two long weekends in two extended *charettes* to finish the proposal.

57. In an extended version of this essay we examine the following projects and other projects more closely.

58. In East Harlem hospitals have played a significant role in the development of the community. Mt. Sinai, Flower Fifth, Metropolitan, and North General have appropriated land for their staff for years. Although these hospitals are the principal employer in East Harlem, the housing they have under their influence is usually provided for people with higher incomes than East Harlem residents.

59. The results of HOPE community's development schemes in balance have been very beneficial to East Harlem. HOPE's developments are among the best maintained privately owned housing in the community, providing the neighborhood with ample affordable housing. However, even though the majority of the residents are Latinos, the "control" of the organization has remained in "white" hands and the "leadership" has resisted any changes to promote Latinos to leadership positions in the upper management of the agency.

60. The circumstances surrounding Pueblo Nuevo's demise remain unclear. However, there was an investigation centered around missing funds.

61. For many years it was commented that Taíno Towers "sucked" the life from its immediate neighborhood by providing an enormous amount of housing next to decaying units. It is argued by many that in neighborhoods like East Harlem building these mega-projects can do as much harm as good by creating a centripetal force that prevents its immediate neighbor from development.

62. Choosing the "technical team" which included an architect as the team leader was usually a combined decision of the city agency and the developer. This combination all but guaranteed that Latino or other architects of color would rarely be chosen to be at the helm of the team. Beyond these institutional barriers the few Latino architectural firms that had been established in the 1960s faced other formidable barriers, particularly the ones posed by community development agencies, which many times "undervalued" their own, believing many times that white architects knew best. This barrier is still present today.

63. At the time the issue of being a "minority" was not understood by those born in Puerto Rico. Although aware of the colonial status of the island, those who grew up in Puerto Rico and then came to the US, either as students or as workers, were aware of the cultural issues surrounding colonial peoples. However, the experience of the ghetto added other dimensions which those coming from the island failed to comprehend. Thus, to many in the staff, those born in New York City, for example, were always trying to prove themselves. Some finally understood the devastating impact the school system had had in the development of identity to Puerto Ricans in New York and elsewhere.

64. In both Poston and the *Life* article there is mention of the original RGS crew imagining invading Cuba to liberate it from Castro.

65. Robert Halpern, *Rebuilding the Inner City: A History of Neighborhood Initiatives to Address the Poverty in the United States* (New York: Columbia University Press, 1995), p. 118.

Victor M. Rodriguez
Concordia University

Boricuas, African Americans, and Chicanos in the "Far West": Notes on the Puerto Rican Pro-Independence Movement in California, 1960s–1980s[1]

Abstract *From the late 1960s through the 1980s, Puerto Ricans developed a movement in California in support of Puerto Rico's political independence that allied itself with Anglos, African Americans, Chicanos, and other Latinos. These alliances were strategic in extending the influence of the movement in solidarity with Puerto Rico's struggle beyond the relatively small and geographically dispersed Puerto Rican population in California. These implicit and explicit political alliances with other sectors led to an interesting ideological and cultural exchange between radical Puerto Rican organizations and these groups. These notes initiate an exploration of this period, through the oral histories of some of the participants in this movement. The focus of the initial exploration is on those who were in positions of leadership and influence in Northern and Southern California within the radical politics of the Puerto Rican Socialist Party—at the time, the main Puerto Rican socialist organization in Puerto Rico and the US.*

Radical politics in the United States have historically benefited from the skills, traditions, and perspectives that immigrants have brought with them as they create a space for struggle and survival within this society. In fact, radical politics within the US were energized and shaped by the contributions of Russian, Jewish, Polish, Irish, Mexican, Puerto Rican, and other groups who, for various reasons, found themselves as part of the flow of labor this nation has attracted from all over the world.

0739–3148/98/040421–19 © 1998 Caucus for a New Political Science

Latinos, and specifically Puerto Ricans, have made significant contributions to US popular struggles that have yet to be recorded in the history of US social movements. For Puerto Ricans who became part of the *diaspora,* participating in political struggles in a nation that was foreign and hostile to them represented just one more tool for material and spiritual survival.

Within the anthropology and sociology of social movements, movements of cultural reaffirmation and resistance are usually categorized as revitalization movements. Whenever these movements have a religious character or expression they are called religions of the oppressed. These movements tend to be considered pre-political expressions of resistance against the encroaching colonialism of expanding empires.[2] The struggle of Puerto Ricans for independence is neither a revitalization movement nor a religious movement; it represents a clear example of an explicitly political struggle against oppression both as a colonized people and as oppressed minorities within the complex mosaic of US racial and ethnic groups.

This political struggle influenced and is itself influenced by the nature of California's regional history and struggles of working people in the United States, by the complex dynamics of the relationship between Puerto Rico's struggle for independence, and by the political and demographic makeup of Puerto Rican populations in the United States. What makes this political struggle unique and widely misunderstood is that there is widespread ignorance about the continuing relevance of anti-colonial democratic struggles today. Most people assume that anti-colonialism is an anachronism, that somehow we live in a post-colonial world. Most of our models for understanding these struggles hark back to pre-industrial societies or the post-World War II decolonization process in Africa. Puerto Rico and the United States are in an anachronistic colonial relationship similar and dissimilar to the classic colonial experience. In one sense, Puerto Ricans are struggling a 19th century battle against a 21st century superpower. Most victorious anti-colonial struggles were facing declining empires, not a still-vital global power.

In the southwest, and particularly California, Puerto Ricans developed a movement between the late 1960s and the early 1980s that generated solidarity with the liberation struggle of *Boriquen*. At the same time, these struggles were shaped by specific linkages and alliances they entered into in their respective communities. These alliances with African American and Chicano/Latino organizations reveal much about racial and ethnic dynamics in the US, particularly in California, and also reveal some interesting patterns about the limits and strengths of radical political ideologies within communities of color.[3]

Puerto Ricans in California

The history of Puerto Ricans in California provides an interesting contrast with the stereotypes developed in US popular culture. While the New York *barrio* image dominates the understanding US has about Puerto Ricans, this portrait has very little to do with the reality lived by Boricuas in the west. One important factor among many others is that Puerto Ricans in California are part of a social milieu that has a history of Latino presence and influence that is more significant than in the northeast. From Texas to California, a significant Mexican/Latino presence extends itself back into the 16th century.

At the time of the Mexican–American War (1845–1848), Mexicans had developed a small but significant presence in what today is the southwest of the United States. As a result of the war, almost overnight, and despite the Treaty of Guadalupe Hidalgo, Chicanos became foreigners in their own homeland.[4]

Like Puerto Ricans, Chicanos developed independent political organizations to achieve the objectives of community empowerment. Two of the most interesting political projects among Chicanos were the Raza Unida Party (in Texas and California) and the Centros de Accion Social Autonoma, Hermandad General de Trabajadores (CASA-HGT), a Marxist influenced organization that developed strong relations with the Puerto Rican Socialist Party, itself a Marxist–Leninist organization.[5]

African Americans were not newcomers to California, despite the image that their presence in the west was initiated during World War II as labor-hungry defense industries opened their doors to African Americans. In fact, African Latinos were among the founders of "Nuestra Señora de Los Angeles," which is the original name of the city of Los Angeles. But it is true that the great demand for labor as a result of the war effort attracted large numbers of African Americans to California. A significant community developed in a number of places, but the largest were in the Bay Area of San Francisco and in Los Angeles. The most extensive relations between Puerto Ricans and blacks took place in the Bay Area, both in San Francisco and Oakland. These relations included some joint work with the Black Panther Party and other black organizations.

The Puerto Rican presence is relatively recent in California.[6] According to Carmelo Rosario Natal, the first recorded presence of Puerto Rican immigrants took place in 1900 when four to five workers destined for the sugar planta-tions of Hawaii got off at the train station in Ontario and fled into the lemon and orange groves.[7] Later, in December of that same year, another group of approximately 50 Puerto Ricans also refused to be sent to Hawaii and disembarked in the port of San Francisco. By 1906, there was the first "Club Social Puertorriqueño" in the city of San Francisco. In his classic book, *Factories in the Field,* about California's agricultural labor strug-gles, Carey McWilliams mentions the assassination of a Puerto Rican worker during a protest in 1913 over working conditions in Wheatland, California.[8]

Other Puerto Ricans came from Arizona where they had been involved in migrant agricultural labor and then followed the job demand into California. More recently, Puerto Ricans came as employees of military federal installations in the state, enlisted personnel (including many who retired from service and stayed in California) until the 1960s–1970s when the pop-ulation was augmented by a significant immigration from the northeast.

But the story of Puerto Rican migration to the west remains to be told, as most of the research on Puerto Rican communities in the US has focused on their experiences in the northeast, midwest, and more recently in Hawaii. One reason for its relative obscurity is the relative invisibility of the community in a region of the country that is heavily populated by Mexican Americans. Also, this invisibility continues today because there is no particular region that serves as a cultural center of the community.[9] This Latino/Mexican regional culture and other factors impede the development of a strong ethnic identity that provides the foundation for a political organization at the same time that it makes the presence of Puerto Ricans in California imperceptible. This "invisibility" also makes Puerto Rican political organizations in this state rather unique and rare.

Other impediments, however, are linked to the powerful impact of Mexican American culture in this region. Interesting processes of assimilation into the Mexican American culture and experience are patterns that are yet unexplored and that form part of the cultural dynamics of Puerto Ricans and other Latinos in the diaspora. Important Mexican cultural traditions are effectively incorporated into the region's popular culture. Dia de la Independencia, Cinco de Mayo, piñatas, veneration for the Virgin of Guadalupe are all part of a cultural milieu that influences both Anglo and other Latino cultures.

Also, the positive socioeconomic experience of Puerto Ricans in this region has permitted their integration into local societies. This, in turn, has placed obstacles to the ethnic maintenance mechanism so common in midwest and northeast Puerto Rican communities. This becomes a powerful factor that creates the conditions for the need of political alliances with other organizations, particularly those of people of color. Most organizations that have worked on solidarity with Puerto Rico's struggle for independence are multiracial/ethnic in character.

The Demography of Puerto Ricans in Southern California

A crucial factor in political organization among communities of color in the US is the strength of ethnic identity. Ethnicity is ironically strengthened by such factors as segregation (increasing social interaction within the community), poverty, discrimination, lower levels of formal education—in sum, by the kinds of conditions that tend to isolate a group from the majority and that are part and parcel of the "minority" experience in the US. Puerto Ricans in the northeast and midwest have historically supported the development of a significant number of political institutions, including those supportive of Puerto Rico's struggle for independence.

In the west, political institutions of any kind among Puerto Ricans are rare. Ethnic identity seems to be lower than what is experienced in places like Chicago or New York. Another limiting factor, for radical politics at least, is the seemingly larger assimilation of individual Puerto Ricans into a "white" status and away from ethnic-centered politics.[10] What also needs to be further explored is whether this very common individual experience is becoming a pattern for the entire group. While there are counter-trends whose indicator is language use, there might be a process that may be similar to that experienced by the Irish who before becoming "white" underwent a process of racialization, being considered non-white.[11] The Irish, who initially had engaged in some instances of liberal politics as they became upwardly mobile *vis-à-vis* blacks, later became increasingly entrenched in racist ideologies, particularly tinged with strong anti-black sentiment. Among Puerto Ricans in California, however, while the overt racist character is absent, the Puerto Rican community is a very politically conservative community; this conservatism is rooted in the material conditions of their existence in this state.

One glaring trait of this community is the significant rate of intermarriage among Puerto Ricans in California, both with Anglos, Mexican Americans, and other Latinos. While in 1970, nationally, only 20.5% of Puerto Rican males were married to non-Puerto Rican spouses, 48% of California Puerto Rican males married outside their group. For females nationally, only 15.9% married outside their group, while for California Puerto Rican females it was 44.6%.[12]

A recent study indicates that the process of intermarriage of Puerto Ricans has increased dramatically in California.[13]

According to 1992 US Census data, Puerto Ricans tend to marry Mexican origin persons almost as often as whites. In fact, with the exception of Native Americans, Puerto Ricans have the highest ethnic intermarriage rates, with 58.2% married outside of the group. For Cubans the rate is 34.2%, for Mexicans it is 14%, and for whites it is 6.6%. For Puerto Ricans who are married under the age of 35, 69.4% are married outside of the group.[14]

Another factor that has a bearing on limiting a strong sense of Puerto Rican ethnic identity is that, in general, Puerto Ricans have fared better economically in California than in other states. While historically Puerto Ricans have suffered high rates of poverty, Puerto Ricans in California have fared better. In 1975 the Census Bureau report indicates that in the US 1.7 million persons were of Puerto Rican ancestry, with 33% experiencing poverty.[15] The national poverty for Puerto Ricans has increased; in 1994 it rose to 38.7% for an estimated population of 2.8 million persons.

The average national household income for Puerto Ricans in 1993 was $27,917, only 14.5% hold managerial/professional occupations, the median age is 26 years, and only 9.7% hold a college degree or more. The median household income for California Puerto Ricans in 1990 was $30,000, while for Mexicans it was $29,160, Central Americans, $28,000, and for Cubans it was $30,000. In terms of professions, 25.4% of Puerto Ricans are employed in professional and managerial occupations compared to 23.9% for Mexicans, 15.8% Central Americans, and 5.8% for Cubans.

Puerto Ricans in California have higher median household income, are older, have a higher educational background and lower levels of segregation than Puerto Ricans in the midwest and northeast. In fact, Puerto Ricans and Asian Indians in Southern California are the least segregated (from whites) group. These latter characteristics are more closely associated with the majority white population than with Latinos in general.[16]

For example, California Puerto Ricans have higher educational achievement than the national average for Puerto Ricans. In 1990, 14.9% of California Puerto Ricans 25 years or older were college graduates, while only 4.9% of Mexicans, 11.3% of Central Americans, and 16.1% of Cubans were college graduates. In general, Puerto Ricans exhibit some of the most socioeconomic advantageous characteristics that traditionally impede the development of a strong ethnic identity. For example, in the 1970s, during the time period of this study, the percentage of Puerto Ricans in California born in Puerto Rico was lower than in the traditional communities of the northeast.[17] However, many of the participants in radical politics in California from 1960 to 1980 were predominantly college graduates or college students, many of them from the island. Other important differences from Puerto Ricans in the midwest and northeast are high levels of language assimilation and racial identity.

In terms of Southern California, according to Turner and Allen (1997), at least 77% of Puerto Ricans in California expressed in 1990 that they spoke English only or very well, compared to 42.6% of Central Americans, 48.7% of Mexican Americans, and 49.5% of Cubans. This level of language use provides some evidence for their lack of segregation when compared to Puerto Ricans in the midwest and the northeast.[18]

In terms of race, Puerto Ricans appear to be lighter-skinned (or perceive themselves as such). Few Puerto Ricans live in African American neighborhoods, contrary to a more widespread practice in places like New York and Chicago. Only 3% of Boricuas identified themselves as black.[19] The hegemony of Latino culture seems to serve as a buffer for a greater identification with "whiteness"; however, Puerto Ricans have a strong "Hispanic" identification when asked to identify ancestry. Only 49.1% chose white, while 95.1% chose Hispanic (including those who chose white). In contrast, 64.5% of Cubans chose white, and a smaller number, 94.8%, chose Hispanic.[20] In this region the "Hispanic" category has become racialized to such an extent that, despite being an "ethnic" category, people perceive it indistinctly as a racial category.

Today, despite California's Puerto Rican population reaching more than 131,998, its organizational political reality remains the same.[21] However, these numbers are held suspect by many observers. A study done by the Western Regional Office of the US Commission on Civil Rights in 1980 indicated that Puerto Ricans are undercounted. This obviously may contribute and/or may be an effect of the community's invisibility. The report also stated its geographic dispersion as a factor limiting a public presence for this community.[22] Some reports have argued that in reality the population of Puerto Ricans around 1977 was about 350,000, but these figures are considered too high.[23]

In summary, the region's culture, and the Puerto Rican population's demographic characteristics (including socioeconomic status), all have contributed to a very geographically dispersed pattern of settlement with no clearly defined center. These are the kinds of social factors that place clear obstacles on the ability of an ethnic group like Puerto Ricans to reproduce their ethnic identity, organize, sustain, and develop political organizations. However, despite these structural factors, at least during the period of 1960s–1980s, a small but significant movement in support of Puerto Rico's right to self-determination and independence developed both in Northern and Southern California. The social basis for these efforts will be explained in the last section of this chapter.

La Lucha (The Struggle) for Puerto Rican Independence in California

Contrary to the experiences of Puerto Rican pro-independence movements in the northeast, particularly in New York, the history of the Puerto Rican solidarity movement in California is quite recent. New York, since the second half of the 19th century, was the place where many efforts and organizations worked to promote Puerto Rico's freedom from Spanish colonialism and then US colonialism. There are no records, oral or written, of any organizational attempts in California, before the decade of the 1960s, to support the rising movement for Puerto Rico's freedom.

In 1971, the Pro-Independence Movement (PIM) formally transformed itself into the Puerto Rican Socialist Party (PSP). The PSP, a Marxist–Leninist organization, focused significant efforts into organizing Puerto Rico's working class (particularly trade union leadership) and developing party branches among US Puerto Rican communities. The PIM had built a presence in some communities around the nation as a result of some previous work done by the Nationalist Party in earlier decades. While the PSP did not always have a consistent political perspective toward its relationship with Puerto Ricans in the United States, it was the first Puerto Rican political organization to explicitly focus attention on developing a political constituency in the metropolis. The organizing among Puerto Ricans by the PSP also led to some of the first analyses and reflections (later brought into the academic world) of the relationship between US and island Boricuas. Initially, most of the organizing efforts were limited to the northeast and Chicago, traditional centers of Puerto Rican migration.

The Bay Area in Northern California is the site of the longest and most effective efforts in support of the island's liberation efforts. At least since the late 1960s, there were groups connected with the progressive nationalist Movement Pro-Independence (MPI), the organization that preceded the Puerto Rican Socialist Party. This region of California is also the site of other effective Puerto Rican organizations that are mainly social service providers. The Puerto Rican presence in Northern California used to be the largest until very recently; the initial population was made up of people who returned from Hawaii's sugar cane fields during the first decade of this century.

Another characteristic of the Bay Area is its progressive political culture that harks back to its strong trade union history and presence. This regional culture provided an environment where many progressive movements have developed various efforts to effect social change. It is within this social, cultural milieu that the initial efforts to support the growing Puerto Rican liberation movement took hold.

The organizing efforts in Southern California took place during the early 1970s and, while relatively effective for a while, are no longer in existence today. However, in university campuses in Northern California and in San Francisco there are still organizations (e.g. Casa Puerto Rico) involved in solidarity work and in support of the freeing of Puerto Rican political prisoners.

In the following section the history of both centers of solidarity will be briefly detailed using interviews of leaders involved in these efforts during these years. The names of some of the participants are disguised for reasons of personal security. These notes do not intend to be an "objective" historical account but a political perspective about the efforts of a group of Boricuas to struggle against colonialism in the "belly of the empire."[24]

La Lucha in the Bay Area

Previous to the organization of the Puerto Rican Socialist Party (PSP) unit in San Francisco, Gilbert Rodriguez, a Puerto Rican Vietnam veteran, born and raised in New York, came in contact with the Puerto Rico Solidarity Committee (PRSC).[25] The PRSC was an organization with branches across the US whose goal was to support Puerto Rico's liberation. It was a multiracial organization of Puerto Rican students, mostly of working class background, and middle class white/Anglo leftist activists. The organization's leadership was primarily white/Anglo.

Around 1973–1974 Gilbert came in contact with the PRSC, having been radicalized by his experience in the US forces fighting in Vietnam. He was already a supporter of independence, and issues of racism in particular led him into the pro-independence struggle. It is also through the PRSC that Aurora Levins-Morales became part of the cell of the PSP in the Bay Area.[26] Gilbert Rodriguez had been involved earlier in the founding of the party unit in San Francisco. Aurora arrived in San Francisco around 1976 when the PSP cell was already functioning.

Melba Maldonado, a Puerto Rican born in Guayanilla, Puerto Rico who lived for many years on the east coast also formed part of the PSP cell during these years in San Francisco.[27] Melba had been an activist since her high school days in the island. In 1966 she moved to Newark, New Jersey, where she continued her involvement in a local organization. Her activities were focused on civil rights issues around Puerto Rican empowerment. She came into contact with African American organizations, the Young Lords Party, but was not involved with any specific political party. Eventually she became involved with the PIM, which was the political precursor of the PSP. When she came to California in 1977, Melba was already a member of the Puerto Rican Socialist Party (PSP), so she was able to link with the already established PSP cell in San Francisco.

Gilbert Rodriguez was one of only two of the Puerto Ricans in the PSP born and raised in the United States. Aurora Levins-Morales, born in Puerto Rico, had been involved in pro-independence activities for some time. Her father, Richard Levins, is a North American progressive who married a Puerto Rican. He has been deeply involved in the island's liberation struggle for many years since then. Despite Aurora's long involvement in the movement she explains how difficult it was for her to get in contact with the PSP unit given the geographic dispersion of the Puerto Rican community in California:

> I arrived in February 1976 in the Bay Area and tried to get in touch with PSP and it took forever to find them.[28]

One organizational challenge for any group in California is the great geographical distance between population centers; this added to the geographic dispersion of the community makes organizing difficult. There was, particularly at that point in time, little communication between the dispersed Puerto Rican communities of this state.

The PSP unit was organized in San Francisco as a result of efforts from the PSP New York branch, which contacted Gilbert Rodriguez and another Puerto Rican, Pedro Perez, who had been active in the Bay Area. The organizing efforts (1974–1975) were focused on organizing a study circle to develop a nucleus for a party cell in the Bay Area. This study circle later became a full-fledged party cell in a few years. Its membership was made up of students, Puerto Ricans who arrived from the east coast, and Chicanos. Many of its members at one point or another were women, such as Melba, Aurora, Mayra, Maria (born and raised in California), Esther, Hilda. The others like Alex Ramirez and Pedro grew up on the east coast. Gilbert is the only member who was a constant participant in the group for an extended period of time. The fluidity in group membership is a result of the migratory flows prevalent among Boricuas in the US and Puerto Rico. Some changes in membership, however, are also due to ideology and/or the demands of membership in a militant Marxist organization.[29]

The cell was mostly engaged in organizing events for expressing solidarity with Puerto Rico's struggle for independence. However, no systematic grassroots community organizing efforts were carried out. There was a strong reliance on relationships with organizations and individuals to do this solidarity work. Women had a significant role in terms of party tasks, but were not in positions of formal leadership.[30] One exception was Melba Maldonado, who at one point led the cell for some time. But this was true, particularly, in the ideological realm. The "theorists," a significant position in an organization which emphasized "party building," were mostly men. Significant political education efforts took place in order to develop politically savvy "cadres," but these efforts also laid the ground for abstract ideological debates that did not contribute to strengthening the local organization.

It seems that the tight reins that the US party leadership had on its cells limited their potential for developing a more developed local analysis. In other words, most of the work, including the coalition or alliances with other groups, was focused on supporting Puerto Rico's right to independence and self-determination. The issues of racism, unemployment, and poverty, while present in the internal dialogues, were not consistently woven into a local political analysis that could serve as the foundation for grassroots community organizing. For Aurora Levins, the strong reliance on a party leadership thousands of miles away was an obstacle:

> One of the things I remember... was in fact how lit-
> tle we did, there was way too much reliance on the
> word coming down from Puerto Rico or from New
> York and not that much attention placed to what the
> political situation actually was around us.[31]

Aurora left the organization to join the Puerto Rican Solidarity
Committee because she felt the cell was ineffective in doing outreach in the local community. The PRSC had a Marxist study
group that also worked with the Chicano community but
seemed to be more passive about community outreach.

One of the obvious reasons for this lack of community-cen-
tered organizing is that there was a not a geographically centered
Puerto Rican community. Other reasons were the social background of the participants and unstable membership but primarily that the PSP's ideological control implicitly led away from
a grounded local analysis. The ultimate outcome of such an
effort would be the subsuming of solidarity with Puerto Rican
liberation as one of many other tasks in a multiracial, multi-issue
Latino organization. According to Gilbert Rodriguez, much
energy was spent on ideological debates and struggle:

> A great deal of our work at that time specifically
> revolved around political discussions, ideological
> struggles, the reading of Marxist–Leninist texts, try-
> ing to understand the "National Question," trying to
> come up with good theory about what's proper polit-
> ical activity within the body of the beast. What are
> the real political, economic ties between Puerto
> Ricans in the US and Puerto Rico? I would say that
> we tried to study theory and argued and discussed a
> great deal in the attempt of coming up with a pro-
> gram that was relevant to Puerto Ricans around
> Puerto Rican independence in the US that could also
> be directly linked with the independence movement
> in Puerto Rico. We realized that the conditions in the
> US were different than in Puerto Rico.[32]

This does not mean that there was no effort to work on local community issues, but that the focus on solidarity work consumed most of the cell members' energies. The cell participated in solidarity with Chile, workers' struggles, gay rights, etc., but these were ancillary activities that were not central to the party's organizing strategy in the US. Significant relationships were developed with groups like the San Francisco Mime Troupe, Casa Chile, and other local organizations, but these relationships, while they developed mutual solidarity, did not result in increased organizational effectiveness.

In response to a question about work in the local Puerto Rican community, for example, Gilbert responds:

> We never recruited (in the community) any actual "folks." I look at the time as a time where we spent so much time and energy in discussions and arguments and study and meetings for a...producing leaflets and distributing them, having activities that we didn't do the kind of grassroots organizing that you asked me about a little while ago. We just never did that. It was not a conscious effort, it was not a conscious decision; it was a matter of a small group of people who basically looked so much inward that we never got it together to look outward.[33]

With hindsight it is easy to say that in the long run the organization could have been strengthened; obviously scarce resources (both human and material) and ideological factors impeded a strategy that would have led to a deeper grounding of this organization within the community. These Boricuas were working with the only tools at their disposal; there were no precedents to build on, no body of theory to transform and adapt except the obscure writings of early 19th century socialist writers whose experiences were distant, not only geographically but politically, to the reality of building an organization to empower Puerto Ricans. Building a political organization in an advanced capitalist colonial metropolis was a task for which there were no models to follow.

However, the cell was able to build on its own weaknesses to develop relationships with local organizations that multiplied its presence and augmented its propaganda on behalf of Puerto Rico's struggle for independence. Crucial to these efforts were the experiences of some of its members in other Chicano and African American organizations. These organizations included student, community, and political organizations. Members of the cell were active in NiCh (Non-Intervention in Chile), a group supporting the Chilean resistance to Dictator Augusto Pinochet. At San Francisco State University, Puerto Rican students developed alliances with Chicano and Pan-African student organizations. Also, fund raising events were held for the Sandinistas, Chileans, and other Latino groups in the Bay Area.

The organizational efforts with Chicanos, while considerable, were limited by the nationalistic ideology of Chicano organizations like La Raza Student Organization at San Francisco State. Nationalist Chicano ideology considered Marxism a Eurocentric ideology that had no bearing on the Chicano/Latino struggle. The reconstitution of Aztlan could not be guided by a perspective and theory they considered to be part of the oppressive European apparatus.[34] The uniting factors between the PSP cell and Chicano organizations were anti-imperialism and nationalism. However, their support for Puerto Rican independence was peripheral and limited to support for some cultural issues. Individual Chicanos, however, were involved in many of the cell's activities. The Pan-African Student Union and the Chicano organizations did not have a good relationship with each other because of mutual racial prejudice. In addition, Chicano nationalist ideology on one side and the Nation of Islam ideology among African Americans separated these potential allies.

The other important alliances the cell or its members were engaged in were mostly a result of the relationships of one of its members (Gilbert) with African American organizations. As a black Puerto Rican student in Oakland at a time when the Black Panther Party (BPP) had been hit by repression from COIN-

TELPRO (the FBI's counter-intelligence program), Gilbert was involved in joint student work in 1973 with African Americans. He shared a position in the student government with members of the BPP in a local college. The focus of the joint work was in developing an Affirmative Action program to increase black faculty on that campus.

The organizing efforts included direct pressure on the university's chancellor by the student organization. The university's chancellor responded to the student pressure to hire more black faculty by firing six male faculty members, one Asian, five whites, all leftists, and hired two conservative black Southern women. This led to the demise of the movement because the nature of the university's response led to the undermining of the progressive foundations of the movement.

La Lucha in Los Angeles
Los Angeles is a megalopolis that is usually defined as a city without a center. Los Angeles is actually a network of cities and neighborhoods with a very loose sense of identity but with a strong network of local progressive organizations. It is within this region that the Puerto Rican Socialist Party developed its second significant cell in California.

Placido Rodriguez, Ivan Gutierrez, Zoilo Cruz, Sandra Ortiz, Hector Albizu, Antonio Gonzalez, Olga Perez, and others were at various times part of an organization, the PSP local cell, with significant alliances with the Chicano/Latino community. Placido, born in Puerto Rico and a resident of California since 1957, had a long experience in socialist and pro-independence struggles as a young World War II veteran in New York. He had attended courses offered by the school of the Communist Party in New York. He was a student of Jesus Colon, the veteran Puerto Rican community and labor organizer who was one of the instructors in the school. For Placido, the experience in the armed forces was a defining moment in his transformation into a radical pro-independence activist. Ivan Gutierrez, another significant member of the Los Angeles group, also was a veteran, in his case a Vietnam War veteran.

The Los Angeles group was organized with the aid of a New York branch representative who led the organization of the cell. Among the initial members were Sandra Ortiz, who was married to a wealthy Anglo from Beverly Hills, and Placido, both of whom remained quite active for some years. The members of this cell were mostly students, workers, and local residents.

The role of Puerto Rican students, particularly in the University of California at Los Angeles (UCLA), was clearly essential. In the early 1970s, with the arrival of Olga and Jose Perez, the cell received a boost in activity. Initially, most of the activity was in the area of political education. The PSP weekly *Claridad* was distributed in Latino communities and other educational materials were received that gave organizing goals and theory to the new members of the cell.

The level of meetings was intensive at the beginning; usually there were meetings every night, and they went late into the night.[35] Initially there was a strong sense of democracy that pervaded the group which extended their meetings into long dialogues. In addition to these meetings, members had tasks assigned to them: some were assigned to trade union work, propaganda, finances, etc. The task of selling the weekly *Claridad* was one of the most difficult tasks, because selling a paper in communities that were very conservative and non-Puerto Rican was an almost impossible task.

Olga Perez was one of the most active leaders of the Los Angeles PSP unit. As a UCLA student, she became an intellectual leader of the cell and provided some leadership in developing demographic data on the Los Angeles Puerto Rican community. However, the membership became more diverse when the group recruited Latinos and Anglos into the organization: Frank, an Italian American, and Rosa, his Chilean partner, Pedro Ramirez, a Venezuelan, Martin Soto, a Chilean, John MacBride, an Anglo (later it was discovered he was a member of the LAPD intelligence unit), and others who at various times joined the organization.

Later, in the mid-1970s, Zoilo Cruz joined the PSP cell after being involved in the Civil Rights and the anti-war movement in New York. Zoilo was born in Manhattan and had developed relationships with the Black Panther Party in New York. When he arrived in Los Angeles cell membership was rather diverse, although still led by Puerto Ricans.[36]

The initial external activities of the cell were its participation in a demonstration with the support of Chicano and Salvadorean organizations against the actions of the conservative New Progressive Party (NPP), a pro-statehood party in Puerto Rico. These actions led to very positive and cooperative relationships with a significant number of Latino organizations. The main factor that brought people together, according to Zoilo Cruz, was "cultural identity." MacArthur Park was a neighborhood in Los Angeles where many Latinos, including Puerto Ricans, gathered. Music was played, picnics were organized, and political recruiting took place among the crowds.[37]

One important source of financial funds for the cell, in addition to the members' dues, were "salsa" dances. Salsa became a glue that united various Latino constituencies with Puerto Ricans as connectors between the various groups. Most of the relationships at this time were with Chicanos, including the Brown Berets, due to the fact that African American organizations were in disarray because of government repression. Later, in the 1970s, strong relationships were established with Nicaraguan and Salvadorean organizations.

The cell was able to have its own storefront office in east Los Angeles, which led to the need for a source of financial support. A significant number of persons in Los Angeles, Puerto Ricans and non-Puerto Ricans alike, were financial contributors on a regular basis. Also, study circles were organized to politically educate the party members on various themes, from the "national question" to history and theory. Among the issues discussed was that of immigration, which concerned everyone in the Latino community. Activists like Nativo Lopez and Antonio Rodriguez, leaders of the Hermandad Nacional de Trabajadores (CASA), developed a relationship with the cell through these exchanges.

CASA was a Chicano organization that attempted to influence immigration policies, a crucial issue for Mexican

Americans. The organization was an outgrowth of Hermandad Nacional Mexicana (National Mexican Brotherhood), which had been organized in 1951 with the purpose of empowering undocumented immigrants.[38] CASA members were mostly young Chicano middle class professionals.

In fact, the PSP and CASA members shared a similar class extraction. Both were middle class or, in the case of students, aspiring to be middle class. The analysis of Bert Corona of CASA really applied to the PSP:

> Despite their inexperience, these young activists were highly idealistic and motivated. In the end however, they just couldn't do everything. They couldn't operate the service centers while at the same time trying to organize a mass movement and build a revolutionary party.[39]

The first relationship between CASA and the PSP took place in 1973 when MECHA (Movimiento Estudiantil Chicano de Aztlan), a chapter at California State University at Long Beach, organized an "International Conference of the Americas" with speakers that included Alfredo Lopez, a leader of the US PSP branch, and Carlos Feliciano, the pro-independence leader who had just been released from jail. Alfredo Lopez stayed in Nativo Lopez's home in Norwalk.[40]

This early relationship with Nativo Lopez and his brother (who served as security for Carlos Feliciano) served to create good rapport between the PSP and CASA. Later, during the summer of 1973, Jorge Rodriguez (Antonio Rodriguez's brother) and Nativo Lopez were delegates to the World Festival of Youth and Students in East Berlin, the Democratic Republic of Germany (socialist). There they again met with PSP members and developed contacts that took Jorge Rodriguez and Nativo Lopez to Puerto Rico in 1973. This trip also strengthened relationships between the PSP and CASA. Conversations were initiated about party-to-party relationships, including a follow-up trip to New York where relationships with the US branch were established.[41]

According to Nativo Lopez, there was a strong sense of comradeship and identity, given the similar experiences of Boricuas and Chicanos. "Us, as well as those who studied with us, saw in the PSP experience very similar things to what we were dealing with, identity, the 'national question,' were we a minority within the US working class or from the Aztlan nation, or part of Mexico? The debates never ended. This fed the interest in maintaining a relationship with the PSP comrades."[42]

CASA members participated in a major event in New York's Madison Square Garden in 1974 in support of Puerto Rico's independence. In part, through the support of CASA, a mass gathering prior to the activity "Bicentenary Without Colonies" held in Washington, DC, a 1976 event, was held in a Los Angeles auditorium where more than 3000 persons attended. Juan Mari Bras, the PSP General Secretary, came at the behest of the PSP cell and CASA to Los Angeles to aid in the mobilization for the national event in Washington, DC.

This linkage developed and matured until later a formal agreement between CASA and the PSP was reached in July 1976.[43] Juan Mari Bras, the PSP national leader, visited Los Angeles and in a private meeting with Antonio Rodriguez developed some formal principles for the CASA/PSP alliance.[44]

The alliance with CASA was probably the closest political relationship the PSP established in California. The foundation for this alliance was the common ideological perspective (CASA was a neo-Marxist organization), top level relationships between both organizations, and good social rapport between its members. The CASA activists, particularly the Rodriguez brothers, were supporters of Puerto Rico's liberation struggle and had some knowledge of Puerto Rican cultural identity. The social bond between the organizations was the result not only of political dialogue but also of social interaction in political and social events.

This relationship enabled the PSP to extend its image and influence beyond what its small number of cadres could achieve on their own. CASA sold copies of the weekly *Claridad* in Chicano communities and increased understanding and support for the Puerto Rican liberation struggle. The organizations shared speakers in their respective events, creating a public image of mutual support. However, both organizations experienced a decline partly because of their joint espousal of a doctrinaire ideological perspective.

In the late 1970s and early 1980s, politics shifted to the Nicaraguan and Salvadorean struggles. During this period the PSP cell was weakened but was able to maintain a significant presence in a new organization in Los Angeles which attempted to provide a center for Latin America's national liberation struggle. This organization, the Latin American Coordinating Committee ("Coordinadora Latinoamericana"), provided significant support not only to Latin American struggles in Chile, Nicaragua, and El Salvador, but also worked to publicize and educate about Puerto Rico's colonial situation.

The Nicaraguans had a center, "Casa Nicaragua," which served as a home base for many political and cultural activities. In the early 1980s PSP leaders like Pedro Grant, a trade union leader, were brought to Los Angeles to participate in activities sponsored by the Latin American Coordinating Committee. Ivan Gutierrez, a PSP cell leader, was instrumental in representing the PSP and becoming a leader within the coordinating organization. This alliance extended the organizational life of the cell which at that point was stagnant, given its inability to transform its relatively successful public activities into an expanded membership base. There never was a clear strategy of how to systematically utilize the relationships and activities as an organizing tool. There was no explicit process for assessing whether the cell's participation in events or activities strengthened or weakened the organization; decisions were arrived at in an informal fashion.

However, as in San Francisco, the PSP's Achilles' heel was its bureaucratism, petit bourgeois social base, inexperience, and its lack of a strategy for grassroots politics. As Ivan Gutierrez puts it:

> It was very interesting because the solidarity group with Puerto Rico continued doing solidarity with

Puerto Rico but not really doing political organizing work in the community. While the PSP was more involved in direct political issues, it is amazing because the majority of the members who were in the solidarity committee were students who were at People's College of Law. Those individuals tended to gravitate toward the PRSC. While the members of the PSP were from different backgrounds and those different backgrounds were reflected in the political discussions of the organization. There was always a turmoil about achieving goals, how to go about organizing the Puerto Rican community naturally because the working class members would focus on a different focus than students. Students were transients; they really at the end did not care whether the work was done or not, and those of us who were here to stay were looking for more stronger bonds with the community.[45]

The internal debates that took place in the PSP about national issues (in Puerto Rico) tended to have a distorted effect on the PSP's units in the United States. Because some of the members had been active in island cells their focus was not on the US branch but on the dynamics in the island. In some sense many still saw themselves as "sojourners" with no long range plans to establish themselves in California but return to a middle class status in Puerto Rico.

I never thought I would be still living in the United States. My original plan was to study, get a degree and return home to continue my involvement in the struggle with a middle class profession that could sustain me and my family financially. Farthest from my mind was that I would establish roots in the US. Remember, this was the "entrails of the empire," as Jose Marti called the US; I did not want to be a "minority."[46]

Hector Albizu and Ivan Gutierrez became involved in an effort in the early 1980s to revive the PSP cell and initiated political education with some local intellectuals who supported Puerto Rican independence. Ivan Gutierrez continued his leadership in the Coordinating Committee while Hector Albizu became the cell's theorist. Albizu was a student at a UC campus in Southern California. Albizu placed most of his focus on solidarity with Puerto Rico and refining political theory to guide the cell's political practice.

The cell became involved in a very conflictive 1982 PSP internal debate about the nature of a socialist party. The issues of Eastern Europe were brewing, and the cell asked Melba Maldonado to represent the cell in the party's congress in Puerto Rico. The outcome of that congress resulted in the defeat of what was considered the "left opposition" and to the resignation of all Los Angeles (and some San Francisco) members from the party. This ended the presence of any significant presence of the PSP in California after more than 10 years of political practice. In the island a significant number of party activists resigned, which initiated the process of decline of the PSP and its eventual decision to disband.[47]

In some sense, the abstract theoretical perspective espoused by some of the members led to the eventual demise of the Los Angeles unit. They reorganized as the "Circulo Luisa Capetillo" of Los Angeles but, lacking larger organizational ties and support, they disbanded during the mid-1980s. Today, there is no significant organizational practice in support of Puerto Rico's independence.[48]

Conclusions

The experience of these two organizational units of the PSP in California provides some important lessons about progressive political organizing in communities of color in the US. They also present an exception to the trend toward the racialization of Latinos in the US.

First, organizations which have a weak community base like these two in California can benefit from explicit and implicit alliances with other like-minded ethnic organizations. In fact, the efforts and achievement of these two PSP units would not have survived had it not been for these relationships. Second, and most important, is that one must know intimately the social terrain on which one does political organizing.

Despite some attempts to gather data about the nature of the local Puerto Rican communities and despite being led by "scientific socialism," both organizations failed to understand the nature of the communities they wished to organize. Puerto Ricans in California then and now were demographically different from the northeast experience and lived in a state of geographic dispersion. This conspired against the traditional community organizing efforts that were prevalent in New York or Chicago. The root of much organizing is based on the ethnic identity of a group, and this identity in California, given the powerful assimilationist trends, presents an obstacle to efforts among Puerto Ricans in this state.

Third, the social background of a significant number of participants led the groups away from consistently and strategically developing a long term practice and strategy to develop deeper roots in the local Latino community. Students and other members who were sojourners did not have the inclination to develop the kind of organizing practice necessary to develop an organization that would withstand the impact of membership changes.

Fourth, the social background of many participants limited their ability to develop a concrete practice to link the organization with the communities around them. The excessively theoretical, abstract debates and theorizing tended to disarm and overwhelm less educated members who were ironically some of the most important, consistent resources of the groups. However, the role of some members like Gilbert, Ivan, and others served as bridges between various constituencies of people of color. But these had more to do with the character of these individuals than with the political practice or theory of the groups.

Fifth, the centralization and bureaucratization of the PSP, its inflated sense of itself, and its "Stalinist" authoritarian practice also tended to alienate members and dissuade many from joining the organizations. These practices were not carried out consciously but were an outcome of following the PSP party line developed in Puerto Rico and applied in California in spite of a vastly different social, cultural, and economic context.

Finally, with the demise of a larger network of social movements in the US and California that nurtured a progressive culture, organizations like the PSP could not survive. With the rise of Reagan's "conservative revolution" of the 1980s, progressive politics like the one developed by Puerto Rican pro-independence activists withered on the vine.

I also would argue that the groups' inability to nurture in a more explicit, proactive fashion the leadership of women also hindered the organizations' effectiveness. With so many resourceful women members these organizations could have developed a practice that might have rooted them deeper into the community. However, like many organizations then and now, patriarchy was embedded within them. Even while the surviving group was called "Luisa Capetillo" after its split from the PSP, it failed to deal explicitly with a feminist/womanist analysis of gender relations or issues.[49]

What was significant of these organizing efforts was not their weaknesses, however, but that despite all the odds against them (including counter-intelligence efforts) these organizations, thousands of miles away from Boriquen, were able to develop important relationships, educate thousands of persons about Puerto Rico's colonial situation, and keep hope alive for hundreds of Puerto Rican patriots. These efforts took place in the context of a Puerto Rican community that, contrary to the US Latino experience, was not being racialized as a group but becoming socially and economically integrated.[50]

In the words of Placido Rodriguez about the character of these militants:

> What I learned in my PSP experience in California was that among leftists, socialists, revolutionaries, radicals are people with a higher moral character

than those who are not revolutionary. I came to understand the potential of a human being when he truly believes in an idea. Of what he is able to achieve by his belief in an idea! I understand how the Soviets were able to defeat Germany during World War II and Vietnam defeat the US. All of this still leads me to believe that socialism is the solution.[51]

Notes

1. These notes present a perspective that is part of a larger effort to look at alliances that Puerto Rican independence activists entered with other racial/ethnic groups in their organizing practice in the US and the role of culture and identity in these struggles. See Stephen Hart, "The Cultural Dimension of Social Movements: A Theoretical Assessment and Literature Review," *Sociology of Religion* 57:1 (1996), pp. 87–100. The oral interviews provided much insights into these dynamics, but the particular interpretation and any errors arising out of these are entirely my responsibility. Thanks to Gilbert, Ivan Gutierrez, Placido Rodriguez, Melba Maldonado, Aurora Levins-Marrero, Zoilo Cruz, and others whose names must remain undisclosed.

2. See Ron Roberts and Robert M. Kloss, *Social Movements: Between the Balcony and the Barricade* (St. Louis: Mosby, 1974), pp. 81–90.

3. I will use the term Chicano and Mexican Americans to refer to people of Mexican descent who are citizens of the US. The term "Mexicanos" will be used to refer to foreign-born Mexican residents of the US. The term Boricuas refers to Puerto Ricans, derived from the Taino Indian name of the island, Boriquen. Boricua is very commonly used among Puerto Ricans in the US.

4. For a radical history of the subordination of Chicanos, see Rodolfo Acuna's *Occupied America: A History of Chicanos* (New York: Harper Collins, 1988).

5. For information of La Raza Unida Party, see Ignacio M. Garcia's *United We Win: The Rise and Fall of La Raza Unida Party* (Tucson: University of Arizona, 1989); and Mario T. Garcia's *Memories of Chicano History: The Life and Narrative of Bert Corona* (Berkeley: University of California Press, 1994) for some recent analysis of the Hermandad General de Trabajadores (CASA) history.

6. The role of labor brokers in attracting Puerto Rican labor to the United States was made easier after Puerto Rico's economic debacle caused by US policies following the Spanish–American War of 1898; see E. Maldonado, "Contract Labor and the Origins of Puerto Rican Communities in the United States," *International Migration Review* 13 (1979), pp. 103–21; and B. C. Souza, "Trabajo y Tristeza—'Work and Sorrow': The Puerto Ricans of Hawaii, 1900–1902," *Hawaiian Journal of History* 18 (1984), pp. 156–173.

7. See Carmelo Rosario Natal, *Exodo Puertorriqueno* (San Juan, 1983), pp. 74–76. However, a *San Francisco Chronicle* article (December 7, 1900) indicates the train stopped in Pomona and that the workers fled to Los Angeles.

8. See Rosario Natal, p. 85.

9. See E. Hernandez, Jr., "Puerto Ricans: One of LA's Best Kept Secrets," *Los Angeles Times* (October 30, 1994), p. b14.

10. See my article on the counter-trend to this process of "whitening" in "The Racialization of Puerto Rican Ethnicity in the United States," in Juan Manuel Carrion (ed.), *Ethnicity, Race and Nationality in the Caribbean* (Rio Piedras: Institute of Caribbean Studies, 1997).

11. For recent historical literature on the sociological and cultural formation of "whiteness," see Theodore W. Allen, *The Invention of The White Race: Racial Oppression and Social Control* (London: Verso, 1994); Ian Haney-Lopez, *White By Law: The Legal Construction of Race* (New York: New York University, 1996); Noel Ignatiev (New York: Routledge, 1995); David Roediger, *The Wages of Whiteness: Race and the Making of the American Working Class* (London: Verso, 1995).

12. US Bureau of the Census (1970).

13. James P. Allen and Eugene Turner, *The Ethnic Quilt: Population Diversity in Southern California* (Northridge, CA: Center for Geographical Studies, California State University at Northridge, 1997).

14. Allen and Turner (1997), p. 249.

15. US Bureau of the Census, *Persons of Spanish Origin in the U.S.: March 1975*, Series P-20, No. 283 (August 1975).

16. Allen and Turner (1997), p. 231. This pattern is not unusual except it is more intensified (not being segregated from whites) than in the northeast. See Anna M. Santiago and George Galster, "Puerto Rican

Segregation in the United States: Cause or Consequence of Economic Status?" *Social Problems* 42:3 (1995), pp. 361–389.

17. Allen and Turner (1997), p. 113.

18. *Ibid.* In their analysis of census tracts only nine have more than 2% of the residents identified as Puerto Ricans. In the tract where the largest number of Boricuas live they are only 66 among 3540 residents (Sun Valley, eastern San Fernando Valley).

19. *Ibid.*

20. Allen and Turner (1997), p. 85. Only 85% of Panamanians chose Hispanic, while 36% chose black. For Panamanians, Hispanic and black seem to be both racial and mutually exclusive. This group is further along the racialization pattern.

21. US Bureau of the Census (1990).

22. "Puerto Ricans in California," a Staff Report of the Western Regional Office, United States Commission on Civil Rights.

23. *The Third World Population in California. Council of Intergroup Relations,* cited in "Puerto Ricans in California," p. 6.

24. The participants in the interview were Ivan Gutierrez, Zoilo Cruz, Nativo Lopez, Melba Maldonado, Aurora Levins-Morales, Placido Rodriguez, and Gilbert Rodriguez (pseudonym) and Hector Albizu (pseudonym). These individuals are located in various parts of the US and Puerto Rico. I appreciate their generosity, particularly because they provided me with time and patience for this project. Other participants whose first names are used are also pseudonyms since I did not have their authorization for using their full names. Given the extensive history of political persecution against Puerto Rican patriots, it is necessary to protect their identity. For a recent incisive description of anti-independence persecution and covert actions, see Ronald Fernandez's *The Disenchanted Island: Puerto Rico and the U.S. in the Twentieth Century* (New York: Praeger, 1996), especially Chapter 8.

25. Gilbert Rodriguez, phone interview, June 29, 1996, San Juan.

26. Aurora Levins-Morales, phone interview, December 5, 1995, Berkeley.

27. Melba Maldonado, phone interview, July 9, 1996, San Francisco.

28. Levins-Morales, *op. cit.*

29. Since it is outside of the scope of this paper, I am not detailing the organizational and ideological issues which were paramount in leading to the PSP's demise as an effective political organization. The cycle of ideological and organizational crises affecting the PSP in the island migrated to the PSP's branch units in the US. These debates led to many divisions in the party, including one in 1982 in which the entire Los Angeles cell resigned from the party. For a passionate, particular perspective on these debates, see Hector Melendez's *El Fracaso del Proyecto PSP de La Pequena Burguesia* (Rio Piedras: Editorial Edil, 1984).

30. Levins-Morales, *op. cit.*

31. *Ibid.*

32. Gilbert Rodriguez, *op cit.*

33. *Ibid.*

34. *Ibid.*

35. Placido Rodriguez, phone interview, July 31, 1996, Los Angeles.

36. Zoilo Cruz, phone interview, January 15, 1996, New York.

37. *Ibid.*

38. Mario T. Garcia, *Memories of Chicano History: The Life and Narrative of Bert Corona* (Berkeley: University of California Press, 1994), pp. 293–297.

39. *Ibid.*, p. 312.

40. Nativo Lopez, personal interview, November 5, 1997, Santa Ana, CA. Nativo Lopez shares the position of National Co-Director with Bert Corona of la Hermandad Nacional Mexicana.

41. *Ibid.*

42. *Ibid.*

43. *Ibid.*

44. Placido Rodriguez, *op. cit.*

45. Ivan Gutierrez, interview, June 6, 1997, Irvine, CA.

46. Hector Albizu, personal interview, June 6, 1997, Santa Ana, CA.

47. Later, during the 1990s, the PSP disbanded, and a small organization, the New Movement for Independence (NMI), returned to its progressive nationalist roots. It did not condemn Marxism, but it became a pluralist organization with a small, diverse membership.

48. Hector Albizu, interview, *op. cit.*

49. Hector Albizu, *op. cit.*

50. See, for example, the historically specific experience of the racialization of Chicano/Latinos in California in Tomas Almaguer, *Racial Fault Lines: The Historical Origins of White Supremacy in California* (Berkeley: University of California Press, 1994).

51. Placido Rodriguez, *op. cit.*

Gilbert G. González
University of California, Irvine

The 1933 Los Angeles County Farm Workers Strike

Abstract *Although many historical accounts touch briefly upon the ubiquitous Mexican consulates, none to date have delved beyond superficial details of that presence, preferring instead to reconstruct Chicano political history as if it were an experience shaped by factors within the United States. This study reveals that the Mexican governments in the post-1910 Revolutionary era implemented a strategy to influence the political culture and actions of the emigrant community in the US. An important part of that strategy contained measures to influence and develop an ethnic Mexican unionization movement along conservative lines. The compiled evidence leads to the conclusion that the Mexican community forged their experiences not only in terms of the conditions extant within the US, but that their home government followed them across the border seeking to assimilate them into the social relations and political culture of the emerging Mexican state. Mexico aimed at nothing less than developing a loyal and politically dependent emigrant community, a strategy that replicated Mexico's domestic social policy and complemented Roosevelt's New Deal labor objectives, while corresponding to the labor demands of large-scale agricultural interests.*

On June 1, 1933, 600 farm workers assembled at a meeting at Hicks Camp in El Monte, California, some 20 miles from downtown Los Angeles, spoke out, and angrily protested their sense of injustice. A strike was called that was to be the largest in the history of California agriculture up to that time. The Cannery and Agricultural Worker Industrial Union (CAWIU, a creation of the Communist Party's Trade Union Unity League) served as organizers at this first meeting. Ultimately, 5000 workers joined

0739–3148/98/040441–18 © 1998 Caucus for a New Political Science

the rebellion, waging a protracted struggle through June and July. In the end, a settlement was signed and workers returned to the fields. They had been promised just a few cents more for their labor.

The strike merits our attention for several important reasons. It was this countywide strike that first brought the Mexican government into the Mexican farm workers' struggles of the 1930s. The Consul, the Vice-Consul, and his associate, acting under the direction of the Mexican president and other high officials, waged a powerful offensive against leftist organizations involved in the El Monte strike and, subsequently, intervened against those same militant elements that were central to several later strikes that took place in California during the 1930s. Secondly, the Los Angeles County strike demonstrates that, at that time, local authorities facing a farm labor conflict would identify its instigators as leftist "agitators" or such leaders in the CAWIU, rather than grant the underpaid laborers the legitimacy of their grievances. Lastly, the El Monte strike witnessed the rebirth of the consulate sponsored *Confederación de Uniones Obreras Mexicanas* (CUOM), founded in 1927 under orders from President Plutarco Calles. Renamed the *Confederación de Uniones Campesinas y Obreras Mexicanas* (CUCOM), the union emerged as the main Mexican labor union in California in the 1930s. As in the case of the moribund CUOM, the Mexican Consul assumed the position of treasurer in the new organization and held that post until the Consul–CUCOM connection was severed in a heated controversy during the Orange County citrus pickers strike of 1936.

Relegated to the margins of the historical record, the strike has never garnered much attention from labor historians; it occupies but a minor niche within labor historiography. Neither the several journal articles nor the few book chapters that examine the event satisfactorily analyze the political substance of the Mexico–US connection or that of the Mexico–*Mexico de afuera* connection.[1] Beyond the problematic and sketchy treatment looms the near silence regarding critical actions of the consulate and Vice-Consul Ricardo Hill and his associate, Armando

Flores. This study incorporates new data and interprets it within a broader perspective that analyzes the decisive interventions of consular officials and the Mexican government into strikes of the period involving Mexican workers. This approach has the potential to convey a more profound understanding not only of the El Monte strike, but also of the role of the Mexican state within US labor history. At the consulate, two officials, Armando Flores and Ricardo Hill, played particularly significant roles in this strike. Consul Alejandro Martinez also wielded his considerable influence, but it was Hill and Flores who interacted with the Colonia and camps and responded personally to the dailiness of the strike's unfolding drama.

As one of the key figures involved in the strike, Armando Flores had an impressive government background. His presence in Los Angeles colonia activities dated back at least to 1926, and tied him to a militant pro-government and pro-Consul past. Flores first appears in the consulate controlled *Confederación de Sociedades Mexicanas* (CSM), where he held the position of pro-Secretario in the executive committee. Under the influence of the consulate, the CSM spawned the effort in 1927 to establish the *Confederación de Uniones Obreras Mexicanas* (CUOM). His name also appeared on the roster of the founding convention of CUOM, and he was elected Secretario de Actas (Secretary of the Acts) in the first CUOM executive committee.[2] Through his participation in these and other highly visible consulate-generated organizations, Flores gained a favorable reputation among *Mexico de afuera*. Recognized as an experienced labor leader, he delivered addresses at Mexican Independence Day celebrations hosted by the CSM. He was also an avid supporter of the official party, the *Partido Nacional Revolucionario;* Flores organized the Club Pro-Ortiz Rubio during the 1929 elections and campaigned tirelessly for Pascual Ortiz Rubio, the government candidate, handpicked by ex-President Plutarco Calles, Mexico's ruling power.[3] The Club held innumerable community meetings during the campaign and added to Flores' stature as an activist, albeit one closely associated with the consulate.[4] Through his past connection to CUOM, the Club Pro-Ortiz Rubio, and other organizations, Flores had established a wide network in colonias throughout the Los Angeles region. In addition, Flores owned a print shop which, as will be seen, he used for meetings and for printing strike materials.

Vice-Consul Ricardo Hill, Flores' mentor during the strike, and the preeminent consulate figure in the strike, began his service for the Mexican government in 1923. After several assignments, Hill was posted to the Los Angeles consulate around 1933 and named Vice-Consul in charge of the Department of Protection under the supervision of Consul Alejandro Martinez. This responsibility put Hill into almost daily contact with colonia residents, particularly those seeking legal help from the consulate.

Born into a distinguished Sonoran revolutionary family, Hill was immersed in the world of politics from his earliest years. His father, General Benjamin Hill, served as a trusted ally to General Alvaro Obregon, whose forces later triumphed and insured the presidency for Obregon in 1920. Hill's brother, Benjamin, Jr., served as Consul General in San Antonio, Texas during the mid-1930s. Cousin to Plutarco Elias Calles, Hill moved into the foreign service with impeccable family connections that tied him to the fortunes of the ruling revolutionary government. His marriage to Esperanza Pesquiera, of the landed Pesqueira family and owners of the Hacienda Cuchuta in Sonora, further strengthened his ties to the militaristic Calles–Obregon machine of northern Mexico which was to rule Mexico from 1918 to 1934.[5] With the election of Lazaro Cardenas, Hill pledged his loyalty to the new regime.

Wealth and family connections served as calling cards for sinecures, evident in the process that led to the hiring of Hill in 1923. Political alliances also played a role. Documents in the Abelardo Rodriguez file at the Archivo General de la Nación in Mexico City demonstrate that Hill received his post largely due to his father's loyalties to Obregon. Yet Hill had other qualities that made him an ideal candidate for consulate responsibilities. Like many children of the Mexican wealthy, Hill had been groomed for such service through private schooling in Mexico

City and the US. He finished his preparatory schooling at the New York Military Academy, Cornwall-on-Hudson, where he undoubtedly learned English.[6]

As was true of all who served in government posts, loyalty to the president and to the administration's policies was considered paramount, essential to the smooth operation of the consular corps. Hill's conduct during and after the strike demonstrates his full and complete allegiance to Mexico's ruling party. Conventional interpretations misconstrue the roles taken by the Vice-Consul and Flores in relation to the growers and local authorities, portraying the growers as successfully maneuvering Hill and Flores to fit their labor strategy. Scholars have overlooked the political drives organized by the Mexican government, beginning in the early 1920s, in an effort to channel expatriate political activism onto conservative ground. The nationalistic political spadework performed by the government has sometimes been mistaken as evidence of IWW-style anarchism, if not revolutionary radicalism. The Los Angeles consulate had long cultivated a tradition of *Mexicanismo,* a Mexican conservative political consciousness consonant with the ruling party. Hill and Flores were well schooled to carry the conservative banner that had been passed to them. In attempting to subvert leftist tendencies and build a conservative union movement, the two men invoked a narrow nationalistic *Mexicanismo* that was antithetical to the Marxist principles of class politics espoused by the CAWIU. This conservative consulate perspective, born of elitist privilege, stopped far short of the working-class politics that formed the bread and butter of the CAWIU.

Consular intervention receded from the scene in the late 1930s; however, a decade of conservative consular activism in the Mexican labor movement seriously impeded the CAWIU from making inroads among Mexican labor. The farm labor movement, pulled in opposite directions by the conservative nationalist charms of the consulate on the one hand and the appeal of the CAWIU's union militancy on the other, never composed itself long enough to establish its own union agenda.

The Mexican Workers

Mexican migration increased enormously during the first three decades of the century, swelling their population by as many as 1.5 million across the southwest. In the city of Los Angeles the Mexican population rose from 33,644 in 1920 to well over 100,000 in 1930. The county census placed the number of Mexican residents at nearly 200,000, but reliable observers estimated 250,000. These rapid increases in population inevitably led to the development of new settlements. Approximately 30 small enclaves outside of the huge Los Angeles colonia were scattered throughout the county at the end of the 1920s boom. Popularly known as camps, and subjected to the practice of restrictive covenants, families literally lived "across the tracks," a popularly used referent for the "Mexican quarter." Often camps were set up on bits of land that owners had parceled out as rental areas exclusively for Mexican tenants. Described by one observer as "Patches of ground...as small as twenty by thirty feet," these plots rented for one to ten dollars a month. Given the scanty resources at their disposal, renters then built their own homes using inexpensive, second-hand, or discarded materials. Amenities were not provided.

Most Mexican laborers were employed primarily as common labor, and nearly eight out of every ten worked in agriculture. And as the Depression deepened, the trappings of poverty began to seem insurmountable. County truck farmers were also hit hard by falling prices. They countered their dwindling returns by cutting wages for farm laborers as much as one-half. Wages that had been as high as 25 cents an hour the previous year were cut to 10 and 15 cents an hour in 1933. Reducing wages made business sense to the farmers, but to the farm workers, it was the bitterest of pills, impossible to swallow in silence. In the face of this blow, a strike appeared to offer workers a realistic opportunity to reverse the decline. A strike would be a visible signal to the world of the pickers' plight and would force growers to authorize a decent raise in the per hour wage, countrywide. In any case, the laborers who had so little had little to lose since the wages offered were insufficient for survival, even if help from the county relief agency was counted in. The strike was all they had.

The Strike

CAWIU organizers arrived in the El Monte area sometime in the spring of 1933. They encountered a potentially explosive situation in the colonias and camps; laborers rife with discontent were without resources to resist the wage cuts. The cadre began its work and soon attracted enough followers with sufficient energy to mount a challenge to the growers. A petition was hammered out, asking for an increase of wages to 35 cents an hour. There was no reply. It was in reaction to this affront that the general meeting of workers was called for June 1 at Hicks Camp in El Monte.

By the end of the first day of June, the 600 farm workers who had assembled for this meeting, carried on a wave of optimism, had voted a strike unanimously. They had come with their anger and despair to confront the crisis. They had talked and listened to the CAWIU organizers. And finally they had moved to redress the miserable wages by their own actions. Hicks Camp was transformed that night from a quiet isolated colonia to the vital control center of a countywide strike movement. Before the boisterous meeting had ended, an immediate halt to all work in the area was declared. There would be no return to the fields until their demands were met. In the fervor of the evening a 50-man strike committee comprised of Mexican, Filipino, and Japanese workers representing the area work sites took on the task of coordinating and organizing the strike. In a deliberate attempt to widen the participation of other workers, the CAWIU leadership had stepped back and assigned only two of its members, Lino Chacon and J. Ruiz, to the Committee. This strategy (to pull workers into the planning process) was ultimately disadvantageous to the CAWIU; it was, in fact, a fateful decision that significantly stifled the union voice during the first week. The two men were, however, elected to the posts of treasurer and organizing secretary and, with other members, swung into action the next morning issuing leaflets, flyers, and bulletins, as reported two weeks later in the *Western Worker,* organ of the west coast branch of the Communist Party.[7] The strike action spread like wildfire, and work stopped in many sections throughout the county.

Pickets were assigned to various work sites and, according to the *Western Worker,* within a few days "over one hundred of the workers joined the CAWIU."[8] Daily meetings at Hicks Camp, designated as strike headquarters, brought workers together for briefings on the strike's progress. Mass demonstrations were held to rally support from settlement dwellers. Informational leaflets bearing the logo of the CAWIU, printed in Spanish, English, and Japanese, spread news of the strike throughout the county and urged workers to join the movement. From the very beginning, a powerful conservative faction in the strike committee challenged the CAWIU for control and, in fact, threatened the union's very presence in the strike. A disruptive internecine fight for control of the strike ensued. Unknown to union representatives at the time, the strike committee included old-line CUOM leaders, one of whom, Armando Flores, was soon to dominate the committee. Although Flores was a print shop owner and not a farm worker, his consular connection conferred power and prestige. He used both to contest the CAWIU and their followers among the strikers, joined by Vice-Consul Hill with whom he had already established a political partnership. Hill, along with Flores, was destined to play a leading role in thwarting the union.

In the initial days, after El Monte, the strike soon encompassed several thousand workers in widely separated areas of the county. The lines of power were clearly drawn, with the consular coupling of Hill and Flores on one side, and the CAWIU on the other. As events unfolded, the consular emissaries would prove the more formidable foe. Influenced by consular prestige and the establishment's anti-union sentiment, newspaper reports scarcely referred to the union.

News coverage favored Hill and Flores with numerous mentions, heightening their visibility and importance. The very opposite held true for the CAWIU. The union was made to seem isolated from the daily intercourse of the *colonia.* As the strike spread and as incipient labor unions in the form of local committees were established, the tension caused by the two contradictory political orientations at the center of the movement threatened the cohesiveness of the endeavor. However, Vice-Consul Hill and Armando Flores steadfastly pushed their agenda, gaining ground, inch by inch. With consular as well as other conservative powers behind them, the Consul emissaries had the advantage and, with the support of their followers on the strike committee, they began to coordinate the dispersed actions and bring all factions together—except the CAWIU—into one single movement.

Hicks Camp remained the strike headquarters and by the end of the first week Hill and Flores had taken a central position. On June 5, the strike committee sent an official delegation consisting of the conservative faction to consulate offices where they were assured that consular intervention would take their cause directly to farmers' representatives. Later that same day at a meeting at Flores' print shop, presumably of the strike committee, new directives were drafted. With no CAWIU present, these more conservative actions reflecting the Mexican government's agenda (to maintain the existing order), rather than the union's defiant radicalism, were carried forward. First, the committee formed several coordinating subcommittees; second, and more importantly, the committee decided to send an informational memorandum to Mexico's Secretary of Foreign Relations and to the Secretary of Industry, Commerce, and Labor. In addition to informing the Mexican government concerning the strike, the group resolved to seek the solidarity of "labor organizations in Mexico."[9] Finally, they agreed to communicate strike information to Mexican newspapers, and especially Mexican labor journals. It is significant that the strikers turned to their government and, it seems, turned their backs on the CAWIU cadre who had been the instruments of action on June 1.

Within days of the strike call, the consulate, the administration of President Abelardo Rodriguez, and Mexican labor organizations were all pulled into the conflict initially led by the very antithesis of Mexican official politics, the CAWIU. At the same time, formal leadership was swinging inexorably to Flores and Hill. At a June 6 rally in Santa Monica, where both men addressed the crowd, Flores distributed strike bulletins without the CAWIU logo, a power play that made it appear that the CAWIU had been shut out. Significantly, the bulletins had been composed by Flores and printed in his shop.[10] In spite of their determination, and by their own reckoning, the CAWIU continually lost ground within the strike committee and was relegated to working in the wings rather than at center stage. The union's understandable confidence during the first few days of the strike had proved unwarranted. With neither a firm grasp of the conditions affecting labor in the area, nor with the time to effectively build a union, the organizers, outsiders themselves, would soon be on the outside. The CAWIU, being too few and too inexperienced, had occupied a precarious position from the start. But Hill and Flores, recognizing CAWIU influence, determined to fight it tooth and nail. In spite of the fractious infighting that roiled within the strike committee, the strike's rampant energies had pulled in more than 5000 workers, and, by the second week, the work stoppage extended clear across the county.

Hill realized that even a weakened CAWIU would continue to present obstacles against negotiating a swift settlement, a complication that growers and local officials also feared. This fear impelled Hill and Flores to act with all speed before the CAWIU could recover, and they pushed hard during the early days to get workers to negotiate. In spite of their efforts, the CAWIU retained enough influence to thwart the early negotiation drive. This failure apparently taught Hill and Flores that in order to get what they wanted, the CAWIU must be brought down once and for all.

It took just nine days for the inevitable and final rupture between the two factions to take place. During that period the consulate, through the strike committee, had reached to the Consul-friendly Los Angeles Police Department (LAPD), and in particular, to its notorious Red Squad, the main intelligence-gathering agency in the Los Angeles area. Dedicated to subverting and destroying leftist, and even liberal organizations, especially militant labor unions, the Red Squad had naturally directed its attention to the strike and, in particular, the suspect leaders. With the Consul's tacit approval, the Squad had assigned several undercover agents, including one described as a Mexican, to infiltrate and investigate the ranks. A stream of reports kept the police department, and presumably the Consul (and thus Mexico City), informed of the strike's progress. The dossiers on the leftist strike leaders gathered covertly by the Squad presented clear evidence of the LAPD's alliance with the Hill faction. The Squad's surveillance and intelligence reports demonstrated support for Hill and foreshadowed an even more direct involvement in events that led to the ousting of CAWIU leaders and paved the way for a takeover by Hill and Flores.

Among the Red Squad's stream of reports, the one dated June 7 stands out. It offers us irrefutable evidence of complicity between Hill and the Squad. This report was sent directly to Captain William F. Hynes, the Squad's commanding officer, and describes the anti-Communist interventions of Squad agents surveilling a strike meeting being held in the Venice area. The agents first observed "the Mexican consul... advising and directing the Mexican field workers," then proceeded to continue their investigation:

> We... found sixty or seventy Mexicans gathered, and in the midst of their group were two white fellows and a Jewish woman. We listened to their conversation and gathered therefrom that these three were communist organizers... After questioning these three subjects, I informed them that we knew purpose in being among the field workers was not to lend aid and food as they had stated to the group, but that they really were there to create dissension and unrest among them. I warned them to stay away, owing to their affiliation the Communist Subsidiary [sic] organization—Agricultural Workers Ind. Union [the CAWIU]. I then went to the group of Mexicans assembled there in the meeting and informed them that these three people were communist agitators. I asked if they wanted to be led or influenced by any such organizations and they immediately answered

they did not and were not aware that the communists were taking part in the strike movement. I spoke to them regarding a raise in pay, saying they must also take in consideration that the grower himself was receiving very little for his product and therefore was unable to pay a very high scale of wages; *told them that if their consul was advising and directing them, I was sure they would not get into any trouble, but if they were communist led and directed, it might lead to trouble for them, such as deportation, etc.* [emphasis mine][11]

Well informed of the battle for leadership, Red Squad strategy aimed at steering the strike into the hands of the Consul and eliminating the dangerous CAWIU. The intervention, reflected in the Venice incident described above, was at first merely persuasive. But to knock out the CAWIU completely, the Squad would require the participation of the Consul as well as the Hill and Flores faction in the strike committee—and a specific moment to stage the event. Chosen for the coup was a meeting to be held at the Hicks Camp headquarters on June 9, and a careful plan was developed under the direction of the Mexican Secretary of Foreign Relations, Puig Casauranc. With the support of the local police (and presumably the growers), the plan went forward. The ambush, orchestrated by Vice-Consul Hill, engineered the expulsion CAWIU members on the Strike Committee and from the movement. "The expulsion," read a *La Opinión* article, "made in public, was taken at the very moment that Señor Ricardo Hill, chief of the Consulate's Department of Protection, exhorted a large gathering of workers."[12]

As previously noted, there were just two CAWIU members on the Strike Committee, Lino Chacon and J. Ruiz. Both were thrown out and charged by Hill with distributing Communist literature and with "frequently urging militant measures against scabs." Those acts, which had indeed taken place, were tantamount to a crime in the eyes of Hill.[13] Many in the rank and file, but certainly not all, appeared to accept the abrupt action and generally followed Hill's lead. When eyewitnesses described the tense meeting, they showed an almost worshipful respect for their Consul. One laborer was quoted as saying, "Today in the afternoon Señor Ricardo Hill, in whom we have placed all of our confidence, came by Hicks Camp to help us. We told him of the presence of those elements...and since Señor Hill discovered that these men were communists, he expelled them in the presence of all our compañeros."[14]

Although news reports portray the expulsion as a spontaneous decision, we learn that the action was preplanned and had wide ramifications. At least two agencies, the Mexican government and the local police, were integral to the affair. The evidence just presented exposes police involvement in pro-Consul tactics some two days before the Hicks Camp meeting. There is other clear evidence that further implicates the police as participants in the June 9 scheme to effect the expulsion of the CAWIU.

The CAWIU's version of the events alleged (accurately) that some form of collusion between the police and Hill was instrumental. According to the union, the "police posed as friends of the strikers," and the coup began when "on the pretext that the bosses wanted to talk terms, the police lured the settlement committee into the police station and held them there for several hours."[15] In the absence of the strike leaders, the *Western Worker* continued, "the consul called a meeting, denouncing our comrades as 'reds'...and warned them to keep away from the CAWIU. The workers were turned against us." The CAWIU further alleged that Hill promised strikers the protection of the Mexican government on condition that CAWIU members be expelled.[16] The *Los Angeles Times* supported the CAWIU view of the affair. A *Times* reporter wrote that the meeting "was addressed by a representative [Hill] of the Mexican consulate in Los Angeles. The strikers were urged to run the agitators out and were told that when this was done an earnest effort will be made to obtain a settlement."[17] Hill made it clear to the strikers that the promise of government protection was contingent upon kicking out the CAWIU; in other words, the rank and file were threatened with their government's abandonment if they didn't fall in line behind Hill. Note that the CAWIU version cited above verifies that a militant faction continued to operate (albeit with very diminished strength) in the strike movement; and that small disruptive presence served to explain why Hill and Flores would continue their wary watch.

The day after the expulsion of Chacon and Ruiz, as CAWIU forces struggled to regain lost ground at a Hicks Camp meeting, their comeback attempt was suddenly terminated, as police intervened. Some two months later, the *Western Worker* reviewed the raid that had routed the Cannery Union and landed members in jail:

> [Union organizers] were gathered in the [Hicks Camp] hall when the police raided it, arrested eight of them and jailed them. Soon after the Mexican consul again came on the scene.... This time our comrades couldn't counteract his fakery since those not arrested were being kept away from El Monte by the police. The consul then formed his own organization of workers.... Ten days later a so-called "liberal" union was formed.[18]

A different perspective was reflected in *La Opinión*. Immediately after the June 9 meeting, a commission of strikers, led by Hill, appeared at the newspaper's offices "to give an accounting of the expulsion of the two individuals considered communists." As told to *La Opinión*, the strikers praised Hill for his leadership and joined their voices to his. In an article titled "*Ya Tienen Esperanzas de Arreglo*" ["They Now Have Hope for a Settlement"] their comments revealed, once again, the alliance between the local authorities and the Consul: "Now that we have expelled those two 'leaders' the authorities have lent us all their support, indicating to us, in addition, that the movement we have initiated is totally justified."[19] Mexico's Secretariat of Foreign Relations also made marked reference to a notable improvement in "the attitude of the local authorities towards the strikers...probably due to the fact that Communist agitators" were eliminated.[20]

The *Los Angeles Times* reported that at one gathering of peaceful pickets, all suspected CAWIU members were "placed under arrest...as soon as they made their appearance."[21] Predictably, the level of militancy decreased upon the official departure of the union from top posts, and the more "peaceful" non-CAWIU pickets were left alone.[22] Without the CAWIU's feistiness, volatile incidents on the picket lines were less common. Credit for pacifying the movement is given to Consul Alejandro Martinez who had seized the moment following the expulsion by "appealing to them [the strikers] to return to their work at once and settle their difficulties peacefully."[23] Martinez's personal plea failed to ignite a general move back to work, and the strike dragged on, stirred up occasionally by the CAWIU. One day in late June, for example, CAWIU militants created an "incident" by urging pickets to forcibly remove scabs from the fields. Martinez responded to this alarming news with "instructions to the Mexican workers to disperse and not to congregate in the zones where the Japanese fields are located."[24] Responding to Consul Martinez's authority, most strikers dutifully went back to their settlements. In his optimistic July 1st strike update to President Rodriguez, Martinez stressed that "for the moment alarming characters have disappeared" and that "strikers have retired to their respective camps to wait the results of the negotiations."[25]

Police protection arranged between the sheriff, Hill, and Flores also helped hold picket lines within bounds. The June 25 edition of the *Times* reported that an "Announcement of [a peaceful picketing] plan was made...after a conference between strike leaders...the Mexican consulate, and Sheriff's officials."[26] Thus, 25 days after the strike began, the Mexican consulate had stepped in and taken charge. The prestige of the consulate had been brought to bear in the persons of Hill and Flores, whose class and manner commanded the respect of their farm worker compatriots, and whose dedication to the cause of the workers filled them with hope. Further, the strikers had placed their trust in a president who had shown them that he cared. He would help redress their grievances. Even picket lines became calmer, for now as strikers marched, the police maintained a distant presence. And finally, the "agitators" had been consigned to a minor role.

Although an event such as the expulsion would appear to have been authorized by local authorities, a deeper review of the evidence uncovers the specific policy directives emanating from former President Calles and Foreign Relations Secretary Puig in Mexico City. Puig's July 1 memorandum to President Abelardo Rodriguez in which the Secretary summarizes strike events refers explicitly to Mexico City's direct involvement in the consulate's decisions and actions leading to the CAWIU expulsion.

> Consul Martinez (in Los Angeles) explained that the presence of elements connoted as communists among the strikers made the work of the consul difficult, and for that reason the authorities refused to support those elements [the strikers] and the employers rejected any negotiations. *The consulate received instructions to correctly organize the striking elements and procure the elimination of the communist leaders* [emphasis mine].

> On the 12th the consul communicated that the definite committee was formed, the existing conflict settled, and the elimination of agitating elements of communist affiliation.[27]

June 14th was a crucial point in the strike. It was then that the consulate, invoking its full consulate powers, stepped up their involvement and moved from behind the curtain that had cloaked the agency's intense interest and involvement. The first move was to form a new strike committee of non-militant members under Consul supervision. The consulate offices were designated as new strike headquarters instead of Hicks Camp and all strike activities would now be coordinated by the consulate. Further, the Consul ordered that henceforth no transactions other than those of the new strike committee would be recognized as authoritative.²⁸ Thus, by June 14th, five days after the CAWIU rout, the Consul, in consultation with Mexico City, had taken control; Martinez's official approval would henceforth be required before the new Committee's directives could be acted upon. As for the strikers, their journey from Hicks Camp to the impressive building housing the consulate was to take them from their humble community to a proud chamber of power. Federal mediators assigned to the strike observed the change in headquarters that further isolated the more militant workers and symbolized the change in leadership:

> All leaders of the striking Mexicans and their activities had been transferred to the Union League Building...in the offices of the Mexican consul [sic] and the Mexican government was represented by a Mr. Hill, Mexican vice-consul, and a Mr. Marcus, attorney for the Mexican consul who acted as the spokesmen for all Mexicans involved in this dispute.²⁹

"For the first time since the strike began," announced an article in *La Opinión*, titled *"El Consulado Unifica a Los Huelgistas"* [The Consulate Unifies the Strikers], "the Mexican consulate and the strike committee, the two forces in the strike, are working together to gain the triumph of the movement."³⁰ Both consulate and strike committee looked toward Mexico City, particularly General Calles, as well as to Washington, DC, for legal, moral, and monetary support. With the CAWIU apparently out of the picture, the strike now became an overt political dependency of the Mexican government.

In spite of the consulate takeover, with neither side moving toward settlement the strike stalled. Growers nervously sat on their hands, apparently hoping to outlast the workers whose suffering was severe. It was at this juncture that Hill and the strike committee called upon Mexico as a lever to force the growers to the bargaining table to negotiate under US federal arbitration. The consulate generated a flurry of strike messages to Mexico and Washington, enlarging the scope of the outreach movement. In telegrams to the White House, Flores made an urgent request for a "full investigation as soon as possible."[31] Two days later the US Department of Labor's Conciliation and Mediation Service directed commissioner E. H. Fitzgerald to "take up the situation affecting Mexican laborers...in southern California."[32] Fitzgerald interceded, orchestrating over seven meetings with the strike committee and Hill between June 21 and June 25. A formal negotiating session was set for June 26. At last the two sides would face each other as they sat down together at the same table.

At this lone negotiating session, Hill, Flores, Attorney Marcus, and the 50 members of the strike committee represented striking workers, and Japanese Consul Satow and the Grower Association Secretary, S. Fukami, represented the growers. The Association had, in a prior move, offered 15 cents an hour but, after two days of lobbying by the Los Angeles County Chamber of Commerce, had finally upped it to 20 cents which was put on the table on the 26th.[33] The strike committee balked and would not go along with the offer, bringing negotiations to a halt. Pressure was applied from all sides with Hill pushing hard, but the committee was adamant. Three hours of parleying produced no signs that the committee would capitulate; they dug in their heels, "the Mexican group refused to sign."

Thinking they had the growers "on the run," they tried to push their advantage by asking that a general expanded wage gain for workers beyond the county region be included in the settlement. They were mistaken in judging that the growers would capitulate in order to get the strike settled. The growers said no. It was a standoff. Hill's efforts to pull the committee back in line had failed. The strike was on.[34] Los Angeles Chamber of Commerce staff member, Ross Gast, commented in an interoffice memo to Dr. George Clements, head of the Chamber's Agriculture Bureau, that "he [Hill] told me privately that he wanted to sign but could not control the group." Hill was especially frustrated because he had worked tirelessly in back rooms to hammer out the agreement with "the strike leaders, the El Monte Chamber of Commerce, and the Los Angeles Chamber of Commerce" and the growers.[35]

The fact is, members of the strike committee had refused suddenly to give full responsibility to Hill and Flores. Such independence suggests that militant members, though few, still had real power, enough to swing votes. Hill and Flores had apparently been overconfident, expecting to pull off the settlement without opposition, but they had underestimated the activist faction. It was still in business, most surely led by Guillermo Velarde, an IWW sympathizer. The strikers had for weeks pinned their hopes on Hill as the embodiment of the Mexico City connection. They had invited the intercessions of President Abelardo Rodriguez, of former President Plutarco Calles, and of the semi-official (and thoroughly corrupt) labor federation, the *Confederacion Regional Obrero Mexicano* (CROM). Their grand expectations were perhaps not to be so cavalierly extinguished (as Hill argued against their demands), especially not by Hill, whom many of the strikers evidently had trusted. In mid-June communications to CROM headquarters had urgently requested "funds to purchase provisions to sustain the movement." Apparently, such gestures led workers to believe that outside assistance would lead them to the victory for which they had sacrificed.[36]

Eucario Leon, CROM's Secretary General, assured Flores that the organization stood solidly behind the strike. Pleased with Leon's reply, Flores answered in the pages of *La Opinión* that "the institutions of Mexico continue cooperating to obtain the triumph. The triumph will not be that of the Mexican pickers, but of all Mexicans."[37] The voices of the pickers themselves were strangely silent. As Mexico City's power brokers assumed the central place in the conflict, the pickers seemed to recede to the background, and the governing institutions could move as they pleased in order to assure an outcome favorable to their interests. The pickers themselves could hardly be expected to be aware of this underlying agenda, especially when all signs pointed the other way.

The positive news was that CROM had responded to the pickers' pleas. Following the receipt of their response *La*

Opinión headlines broadcast "CROM Supports the Strikers" and reported that a CROM commission scheduled a meeting with President Rodriguez to request "rapid measures to back the movement."[38] Flores also petitioned former President Plutarco Calles, the power behind the administration of President Abelardo Rodriguez. Flores wrote, "Taking into consideration your undeniable sympathy for the agricultural laborers, we respectfully implore whatever help possible to sustain the strike."[39] The message assured Calles of "our gratitude for material and moral support."[40] Calles responded favorably to Flores' petition and the next day wired $150 by way of the consulate. Two days later he sent another $600. From El Sauzal, his resort-like hacienda in Ensenada, Calles began to orchestrate Mexican activities linked to the strike, and even the strike itself, no matter that it was unfolding in the US.

Word of Calles' support reached deep into the colonias and camps, and Calles emerged a hero among the strikers and in the worker settlements where shouts of "Viva el General Calles" reverberated through the paths and streets of these strife-torn places. One leader described Calles as "a great friend and defender of the working class" and "high protector of the working class."[41]

Actions and messages from Secretary Puig had further encouraged the pickers. Puig expressed his government's interest in the strike to US Ambassador Josephus Daniels, thoughtfully pointing out that all radicals had been expelled, and requesting that Washington intervene on behalf of the strikers. A *La Opinión* article reported that Puig not only declared the Mexican government's support, but added that $1000 was to be sent to the Los Angeles consulate as a demonstration of the president's cooperation.[42] In total, the monies originating in Mexico and sent to the consulate for disbursement to the strike committee came to more than $4000; Calles personally sent over $1000. All this activity took place prior to the negotiations on June 26. It might be assumed that such impressive high-level maneuvering would have raised the hopes of the strikers and thus been a factor in their decision to reject the growers' wage offer.

It is commonly assumed in political circles in and out of Mexico that Calles openly pulled the strings at the president's office and at the Secretariat of Foreign Relations. Certainly, the stream of strike information flowing back and forth between Mexico City and Los Angeles always reached Calles' headquarters and this personal involvement strongly implicates him in decisions and activities that would affect the strike's outcome. A special memorandum on the state of the strike prepared by Puig for President Rodriguez reflected on Calles' role in the support movement. In that memo Puig quotes from his previous wire to Calles: "With pleasure I write, my General, that from the beginning of the strike this Secretariat has been in constant contact with the striker's committee, and the CROM Executive Committee has given absolute support to the movement."[43] In a later telegram sent from the president's office to Consul Martinez, Puig acts as go-between, passing on Calles' enthusiastic evaluation as well as congratulations on following the president's "orders": "Señor General Calles congratulates the Secretariat [of Foreign Relations] and you for your efficacious and patriotic labor undertaken in the strike of Mexican workers, *thus complying with the orders transmitted from the President via this Secretariat*" [emphasis mine].[44]

Technically, the evidence available—letters, memoranda, telegrams, news coverage—leaves no doubt as to the involvement and direct intervention in the strike of the Mexican government. Calles, the government of Mexico, and the ruling party, the *Partido Nacional Revolucionario* (PNR), can be seen as one political entity, and it is Calles' support that made him into the hero the strikers needed. So strong were the feelings Calles aroused among the striking pickers that they informally honored him with the title "Father of the Movement."[45] Nevertheless, in spite of the Calles support, the hot summer month of July began without a settlement on the horizon. In Mexico, Calles, the PNR, President Rodriguez, and CROM forged ahead, organizing nationalist propaganda in defense of the strike. Calles issued telegrams in late June to Luis L. Leon, the editor of the official government's (and PNR) newspaper, *El*

Nacional, and to the PNR president, General Manuel Perez
Trevino, urging their collaboration with the support campaign.
CROM responded to the strikers' pleas by directing that all affil-
iates back the strike.

As July began the strike lingered on, perhaps, in part,
because pickers continued to believe that their government
would lead them to victory. For those in authority, the time had
come to close off the strike; patience had run out. From Mexico
City came the word, a directive that would resolve the impasse.
On July 4 Consul Martinez received his instructions from
President Rodriguez: "I deem it advisable," stated the president,
"that you actively resolve the strike at the earliest."[46] Martinez
immediately responded, informing President Rodriguez via
phone that "in his estimation a 20 cents per hour offer was sat-
isfactory." This response, with an exact per hour figure, makes it
clear that Consul Martinez had conferred privately with the
growers to discuss a wage settlement agreeable to them before
convening a new negotiating session with the strikers. Since
Martinez made no mention of the opinion of the strikers as to
the wage offer, we can assume that either their known views did
not enter into his calculations, or the strike committee was not
consulted.[47]

The new negotiating session took place on July 6. But the
pre-selected 20-cent figure was not used in the final arbitration.
The two sides agreed to 16.5 cents per hour (or $1.50 per nine-
hour day) for "steady workers" and 20 cents per hour overtime;
temporary workers were to receive 20 cents per hour. It was an
interim settlement whose terms would be in effect for 30 days
and renegotiated on August 15. The signing, witnessed by
Consul Martinez, increased salaries by a few cents but, ironically, lowered the amount (by 3.5 cents) offered by the Growers
Associations at the failed June 26 negotiating session.
Nevertheless, workers went back to the fields—under a new
union. On July 15, the CROM affiliated *Confederacion de
Uniones Campesinas y Obreras Mexicanas* (CUCOM), born during the confrontation with the CAWIU, as cited earlier, celebrat-
ed its organizing convention. The Cannery Union moved on.

In spite of the minimal gains, Armando Flores, the first Secretary General of CUCOM, praised the settlement. *La Opinión* reported that "don Armando Flores, who since the beginning of the strike became its leader...considers yesterday's agreement Mexican labor's biggest triumph in the strike movements of the United States."[48] Consul Martinez also received favorable comments for his role. Deputy Thomas Barker of the State Division of Labor and Law Enforcement praised Martinez for having provided "splendid aid and cooperation" during the negotiations.[49] Hill also received his measure of accolades. A *La Opinión* journalist revisited the strike a year later and, in his report, reminded readers that among the consulate officials, Hill enjoyed the highest regard and affection among industrial labor and agricultural workers in the state of California. In the journalist's opinion, "the most salient person among the Mexican representatives in this city, Hill worked tirelessly among those in continuous contact with him, his prestige would come to have unanimous recognition, when eighteen thousand [sic] pickers declared the largest strike by Mexican citizens in California."[50]

In its congratulatory message, Mexico's government laid to rest any doubts regarding the lines of authority. The Official Bulletin of the Secretariat of Foreign Relations announced that:

> Upon the termination of the strike movement, General Calles, through the Ministry of Foreign Relations, congratulated Consul Martinez and Vice Consul Hill. *The Ministry of Foreign Relations pointed out that the effective and patriotic labors of these men had been carried on in compliance with orders from the President of the Republic* [emphasis mine].[51]

General sentiment placed responsibility for defeating the growers on the shoulders of the Mexican government. "The victory," stated a journalist in *La Opinión*, "without doubt was reached thanks to the decided cooperation offered by the Mexican government, the labor associations of the country, and in particular General Plutarco Elias Calles who, from his residence in El Sauzal, sent large donations of money for sustaining the movement."[52] As was to be expected, the CAWIU viewed the government's role with disdain and attacked the agreement as a traitorous and one that gained the workers little for their sacrifices. One defiant faction on the strike committee, led by Guillermo Velarde, an IWW sympathizer and CUCOM Under Secretary, bitterly assailed the settlement, charging that it was a "sellout." So angered did Velarde become that he turned with finality against Hill and "stopped coming to the [consulate] office."[53] Flores lauded the agreement, and adding his voice to others, proclaimed that Mexican institutions and leaders had saved the strike from defeat. Flores emphatically declared the wage agreement a victory and credited the triumph to the Mexican government. The workers were not mentioned, much less thanked for their sacrifices. "If General Calles had not intervened in our favor," Flores exclaimed, "sending money to help the strikers' families, the movement unequivocally would have failed."[54]

Thus, credit was given where credit was due. But was it? Calles' motives give us pause and deserve closer scrutiny. The Los Angeles Chamber of Commerce contended that the Machiavellian Calles saw an opportunity to recoup political ground vis-à-vis his contenders by posing as a defender of Mexico and its working class. His political fortunes most surely motivated Calles, and little evidence exists that he ever distinguished himself as a defender of working-class interests.

Although the CAWIU had been eliminated in this strike, in large measure as a result of consular directives, the Chamber of Commerce nonetheless misconstrued the roles played by Hill and Flores in the strike and expressed grave doubts about the two officials. The Chamber failed to appreciate that without Hill at the helm, the Cannery Union would surely have exacerbated the labor struggle. Hill, and Martinez, were determined to end the strike through arbitration and appeals to Mexican patriotism. However, the strike was like a monster with two heads; it was impossible to lead in a single direction. The level of militancy forced Hill, correctly as it turned out, to ride out the storm, until he could rid the strike of leftist influence and bring the workers to settle with the growers. The Chamber misread Hill's pragmatic approach which took time, and viewed it instead as evidence of Hill's desire to continue the strike. Clements and the Chamber, in blaming Hill and Flores for prolonging the strike, may have been creating a smoke screen to cover up their own poor handling of the strike, but in any case they were, of course, wide of the mark in faulting the two consulate officials. Hill's alliance with the strikers and his cheerleader rhetoric may have been interpreted as an incitement to worker belligerence, but his motives were as pure as those of Clements; only their methods as to reaching a settlement differed.

Notwithstanding the complexity and ambiguity of these issues, the Chamber decided to address a grievance to Washington, requesting a Department of Justice investigation of Hill's involvement. Clements spelled out the complaint to his superior, Mr. Arnoll, the Secretary and General Manager for the Chamber. He alleged that CROM and the Mexican government directed "Mexican consular offices" to interfere and "organize the Mexican people and agitate." He pressured Arnoll to "Call the attention of Washington and request that the Department of Justice" make an investigation.[55]

The complaint went to the Department of State with the request that the matter be forwarded to the Department of Justice. Rather than involving Justice, State chose to keep the issue as quiet as possible and maintain the matter under their purview. State's Division of Mexican Affairs reviewed the charge and their preliminary evaluation found that "little actual evidence" of "improper intervention" had been submitted.[56] In further discreet investigation, officials concluded that no action be taken "without more conclusive evidence than we now have that Mexican intervention in the dispute was of a character which might be held either unlawful, unfriendly, or improper."[57]

Several months after the strike reached a closure, a communiqué issued by Ambassador Daniels to Secretary of State

Hull commented on a Mexican Foreign Office bulletin reviewing in detail the actions taken by the Mexican government in the
strike. Daniel's comment reflected what appeared to be the State
Department's official opinion regarding Mexico's (and Hill's)
conduct. The communiqué dismissed any basis for charges of
misconduct by suggesting that the Mexican Foreign Office bulletin "need not be read unless you are interested in the matter."
Daniels continued:

> The dispute appears to have been settled . . . . The bul-
> letin describes in great detail the various steps taken
> by the Mexican Foreign Office to support its nation-
> als in California . . . . My impression is that its princi-
> ple purpose was to demonstrate to the Mexican
> people the efficiency and vigor with which the
> Mexican government protects its nationals living in
> even so powerful a country as the US.[58]

The US State Department accepted the Mexican government's
narrow and disingenuous view that its actions were directed
solely at protecting the interests of its citizens living abroad. The
State Department recognized the difference between hostile
nationalism harmful to US interests and that benevolent
nationalism exhibited by the Mexican State. Mexico's skillful
manipulation of nationalist rhetoric barely concealed a corpo-
ratism adapted to US economic and political domination.
Mexico, in its subordinate role, had bowed to US policy, foreign
and domestic. The State Department could afford to uphold the
larger view that as long as conservative objectives grounded
consular activities, the strike and its nationalist appeals merited
minor attention. State Department officialdom had no reason
to bother penetrating the veneer of Mexican "nationalism" to
see the condition it masked. As for the Mexican hierarchy in
thrall to the US, perhaps they could defer to the saying, "so close
to the United States and so far from God." And so when it came
to their compatriots abroad—they were indifferent. Perhaps the
"sellout" of the Mexican workers, or at the very least Mexico's

refusal to stand by them, can be seen on the very deepest plane as a sellout of their own nation.

Notes

1. Rodolfo Acuña, *Occupied America: A History of Chicanos* (New York: Harper and Row, 1981); Francisco Balderrama, *In Defense of La Raza: The Los Angeles Mexican Consulate and the Mexican Community, 1929 to 1936* (Tucson: University of Arizona Press, 1982); Clete Daniel, *Bitter Harvest: A History of California Farm Workers, 1870–1941* (Berkeley: University of California Press, 1981); Ronald W. Lopez, "The El Monte Berry Strike of 1933," *Aztlan: Chicano Journal of the Social Sciences and the Arts* (Spring 1970), pp. 101–14; Douglas Monroy, "Anarquismo y Comunismo: Mexican Radicalism and the Communist Party in Los Angeles During the 1930s," *Labor History* 24:1 (1983); Charles B. Spaulding, "The Mexican Strike at El Monte, California," *Sociology and Social Research* 18 (1934), pp. 571–80; Devra Weber, "The Organizing of Mexicano Agricultural Workers: Imperial Valley, and Los Angeles, 1928–1934, An Oral History Approach," *Aztlan* 3:2 (1973); Charles Wollenberg, "Race and Class in Rural California: The El Monte Berry Strike of 1933," *California Historical Quarterly* LI (Summer 1974), pp. 155–64; Abraham Hoffman, "The El Monte Berry Strike, 1933: International Involvement in a Labor Dispute," *Journal of the West* XII (January 1973), pp. 71–84.

2. "El Consul Pesqueira Dejo Ya Organizado La Surcursal de la CROM en Los Angeles," *La Opinion* (December 12, 1927); also see Governor C. C. Young's Fact Finding Committee, *Mexicans in California*, p. 126.

3. "Una Asamblea Ortiz Rubista," *La Opinión* (September 7, 1929).

4. "Celebrara el 16 en Los Angeles El Ortizrubismo," *La Opinión* (September 14, 1929).

5. Archivo General de la Nación, Mexico City, Ricardo Hill File, Document 21-6-4.

6. *Ibid.*

7. "Raspberry and Potato Pickers Answer the Call," *The Western Worker* (June 12, 1933).

8. *Ibid.*

9. "Apoyan el Movimiento en El Monte," *La Opinión* (June 6, 1933).

10. "Tres Lideres Capturados en Sawtelle," *La Opinión* (June 7, 1933).

11. US Senate Subcommittee of the Committee of Education and Labor, *Hearings, Violations of Free Speech and the Rights of Labor*, 76th Congress, Part 64 (Washington, DC: US Government Printing Office, 1940), p. 23629.

12. "Ya Tienen Esperanzas de Arreglo," *La Opinión* (June 10, 1933).

13. *Ibid.*

14. *Ibid.*

15. "Indignation Grows at Sell Out by Mexican Consul, Labor Dept.," *The Western Worker* (August 7, 1933).

16. "Ranks of Southern California Berry Strikers Solid," *The Western Worker* (August 7, 1933).

17. "Berry Strike Gets Violent," *Los Angeles Times* (June 10, 1933).

18. "Indignation Grows at Sell Out by Mexican Consul, Labor Dept.," *The Western Worker* (August 7, 1933).

19. "Ya Tienen Esperanzas de Arreglo," *La Opinión* (June 10, 1933); "Action to End Strike Begun," Los Angeles Times (July 1, 1933).

20. Josephus Daniels to the Honorable Secretary of State (June 23, 1933). National Archives (NA), Record Group (RG)59, Records of the Department of State, 511.5045/129.

21. "Seven in Berry Strike Jailed," *Los Angeles Times* (June 11, 1933).

22. "Plagian a Siete Huelgistas en El Monte," *La Opinión* (June 11, 1933).

23. "Seven in Berry Strike Jailed," *Los Angeles Times* (June 11, 1933).

24. "Action to End Strike Begun," *Los Angeles Times* (July 1, 1933).

25. Consul Alejandro Martinez to President Abelardo Rodriguez (July 1, 1933). Archivos Generales de la Nación (AGN), Mexico City, Abelardo Rodriguez, File 561-4/18.

26. "Farm Strikers to Start Drive," *Los Angeles Times* (June 25, 1933).

27. Memorandum from Dr. J. M. Causaranc to President Abelardo Rodriguez (July 1, 1933). AGN, Abelardo Rodriguez, File 561-4/18.

28. "Expectacion Hoy Cesa el Ultimatum," *La Opinión* (June 12, 1933).

29. E. L. Fitzgerald and E. P. Marsh to Director H. L. Kerwin (July 3, 1933). NA, RG 280 FMCS File 170/8983.

30. "El Consulado Unifica a Los Huelgistas," *La Opinión* (June 13, 1933).

31. Armando Flores to President Franklin D. Roosevelt (June 14, 1933). NA, RG 280 FMCS File 170/8983.

32. H. L. Kerwin to Consul Martinez (June 21, 1933). NA, RG 280 FMCS File 170/8083.

33. *Hearings,* Part 53, p. 19487.

34. Commissioners W. H. Fitzgerald and E. P. Marsh to Director H. L. Kerwin (June 27, 1933). NA, RG 280 FMCS File 170/8083.

35. E. H. Fitzgerald and E. P. Marsh to Director H. L. Kerwin (July 3, 1933). NA, RG 280 FCMS File 170/8083.

36. "Otro Llamado del Comite de la Huelga," *La Opinión* (June 16, 1933).

37. "Envian un Mensaje al Presidente," *La Opinión* (June 16, 1933).

38. "La CROM da Apoyo a los Huelgistas," *La Opinión* (June 18, 1933).

39. "Calles Envia Dinero a los Huelgistas," *La Opinión* (June 21, 1933).

40. *Ibid.*

41. *Ibid.*

42. "Gran Interes por la Huelga de Pizcadores," *La Opinión* (June 24, 1933).

43. Memorandum from Secretary J. M. Puig to President Abelardo Rodriguez (July 1, 1933). AGN, Abelardo Rodriguez, File 561-4/18.

44. Consul Alejandro Martinez to President Abelardo Rodriguez (July 9, 1933). AGN, Abelardo Rodriguez, File 561-4/18.

45. "Dos Representantes de Mister Rolph Investigan Desde Ayer el Movemiento," *La Opinión* (July 1, 1933).

46. President Abelardo Rodriguez to Consul Alejandro Martinez (July 4, 1933). AGN, Abelardo Rodriguez, File 561-4/18.

47. Francisco Gaxiola to President Abelardo Rodriguez (July 7, 1933). AGN, Abelardo Rodriguez, File 561-4/18.

48. "Los Pizcadores Ganaran 20cts La Hora, Como Minimo, $1.50 Por Dia," *La Opinión* (July 7, 1933).

49. Frank G. MacDonald to Mr. V. Cuevas Lopez, Secretary General, Council of Labor, Tampico, Mexico (July 19, 1933). NA, RG 59 811.5045/140.

50. "D. Joaquin Terrazas Consulen N. Orleans," *La Opinión* (July 20, 1935).

51. Official Bulletin of the Ministry of Foreign Affairs [sic] (translation), in Josephus Daniels to Honorable Secretary of State (August 25, 1933). NA, RG 59, 811.5045/142.

52. *Ibid.*

53. Devra Weber, "The Organizing of Mexicano Agricultural Workers: Imperial Valley and Los Angeles 1928–1934, An Oral History Approach," *Aztlan* 3:2 (1973), p. 331.

54. "Volvieron al Trabajo 6000 Huelgistas," *La Opinión* (July 8, 1933).

55. Dr. Clements to Mr. Arnoll (July 20, 1933). NA, RG 59, 811.5045/139.

56. Unsigned note to Mr. Johnson (July 22, 1933). NA, RG 59, 811.5045/139.

57. H. S. Bursley to Mr. Johnson (July 28, 1933). NA, RG 59, 811.5045/139.

58. Unsigned note in response to the Mexican Office of Foreign Affairs Bulletin, Department of State (September 2, 1933). NA, RG 59, 811.5045/142.

Edna Bonacich
University of California at Riverside

Latino Immigrant Workers in the Los Angeles Apparel Industry

Abstract *The apparel industry is one of the most globalized industries in the world. Apparel manufacturers are moving production to areas of the world where they can obtain the lowest wage labor. Imports of clothing to the US have risen dramatically, while garment jobs have dwindled. Los Angeles is the one area of the country that is running counter to this trend, in part because of its access to a large, Latino workforce, many of whom are undocumented. This paper considers the organization of the apparel industry in Los Angeles today, especially the return of sweatshops. It examines the role of Latino immigrants as operatives in the industry and the conditions under which they must work. The fundamental problem lies in the lack of political power of these workers, who must labor under an apartheidlike system that denies them basic civil rights. Even recent signs of growing Latino political mobilization cannot bring immediate relief. Garment workers need to unionize in order to protect themselves. The problems and prospects for organizing are briefly considered.*

The apparel industry is one of the most globalized industries in the world.[1] The search for ever cheaper sources of labor offshore has led both to a decline in domestic apparel employment and to a rise in sweatshop production based on the exploitation of immigrant labor. Los Angeles has become the premier center of apparel production in the United States, relying heavily on the employment of Latino immigrant workers, many of whom are undocumented.

The purpose of this paper is to examine the development of Latino-employing sweatshops in Los Angeles. I want to understand why this is happening, and what can be done about it.

0739–3148/98/040459–15 © 1998 Caucus for a New Political Science

The US Apparel Industry

The apparel industry in the United States is declining. Every month new reports are put out enumerating the loss of jobs. Meanwhile, parallel numbers report the monthly rise of imports. However, even though apparel jobs are moving offshore, US-based manufacturers and retailers still play a critical role in the production of apparel for the US market. They have become multinational corporations. They now arrange for the production of their clothing in other countries, but they still remain in charge of ordering and marketing.

Unlike most multinational corporations with subsidiaries in developing countries, US apparel firms usually do not purchase their own offshore plants. Instead, most develop arm's-length transactions with offshore contractors and licensees. The contractors produce the goods to be shipped back to the US as imports, under specifications by the US manufacturers and retailers. The licensees are more likely to produce for the local (offshore) market, paying the parent company royalties for the use of their brand name and producing goods that meet the standards of the parent.

The driving force behind moving offshore is undoubtedly the search for lower wage labor. US apparel firms scour the world for the best deals that they can get. In general, they are moving to countries where peasants are being pushed off the land, and where very young women are being forced to enter the paid labor force as a first generation proletariat. These workers can suffer from multiple forms of control and oppression, including patriarchal family relations, brutal employers, and governments that deny their basic political rights. They are the most exploitable workers in the world. For many countries eager to industrialize, the apparel industry provides a first step as a low capital, labor intensive industry. Governments promise US apparel manufacturers and retailers a controlled, trouble-free workforce for a fraction of US wages. Of course, not all US companies choose to move offshore, but the trend is for more of them to shift at least some of their production out of the country. Of the $178 billion spent on apparel in the United States in

1995, over half, or $91 billion, was spent on imports, a figure that keeps rising each year.[2]

The North American Free Trade Agreement (NAFTA) has channeled some of this movement in the direction of Mexico. NAFTA's purpose, in part, was to enable US apparel manufacturers and retailers to rely less on Asia and to develop their "own" low wage labor force within the Western hemisphere. As a consequence, apparel imports from Mexico have soared, overtaking the major Asian exporters to the US and promising to continue rapid growth.

Los Angeles: The Great Exception
In contrast to the rest of the United States, apparel employment has been growing in Los Angeles. Between 1993 and 1997 the LA industry added an estimated 26,000 new jobs.[3] The LA industry is now the largest apparel employer in the United States. True, New York still remains the chief fashion center of the nation, but jobs have shifted away from that city. Moreover, apparel is the largest manufacturing industry in Los Angeles, having surpassed the aerospace industry in the face of post-Cold War military cutbacks. Apparel officially employs about 120,000 people in LA County, and the real number is much larger because of a substantial underground economy.

Los Angeles is mainly a center for the production of moderately priced, fashionable sportswear for women, especially young women or "juniors." LA's garments tend to be geared toward the spring and summer seasons. They are gaily colored, imaginative, reflecting the city's image of sunshine, beaches, and informality. Some of the major apparel manufacturers are: Guess? Inc, Bugle Boy, Rampage, Carole Little, Chorus Line, and BCBG.

Not all LA apparel manufacturers do their production in Los Angeles. Some of them have almost all of their clothing produced offshore, while others outsource part of their production. However, some non-LA manufacturers have their production done in Los Angeles. Even if they produce their garments in Los Angeles, few manufacturers (or retailers) do their own production in-house. They make use of contractors, often many of them. There are literally thousands of garment contractors in Los Angeles, spread out across the basin. Most contractors are small businesses, employing an average of 35 workers, but some employ over 100. These firms are typically assembly plants where workers sit at sewing machines and stitch together the cut materials that make up garments.

The Advantages to Manufacturers in the Contracting System
The contracting system is touted by manufacturers for the flexibility it provides. Apparel manufacturing is unstable, since it is affected both by seasons and by shifts in fashion. The contracting system enables manufacturers to have work done only when they need it, thereby avoiding the maintenance of a stable labor force that they do not need year round. The contractors are able to absorb the changing demands of the industry, shifting their work among different manufacturers in an effort to keep their factories running at full capacity.

But there is another side to the contracting system. It also serves as a labor control system. The contractors typically do the sewing or assembly. Some contractors specialize in cutting, laundering, or finishing, but the majority are assembly plants. By contracting out, the manufacturers externalize the labor. The manufacturers never lose title to the goods that the contractors sew. They do not sell the cut goods to the contractors. Instead, the contractors basically supply only the labor. They are essentially labor contractors.

As we have said, most contractors are small businesses. They are typically run by immigrant entrepreneurs who usually do not have much capital. Manufacturers are able to pit contractors against one another as they underbid each other to get the work. Contractors are typically offered a price for the work on a "take it or leave it" basis, because the manufacturer can always find another contractor who would be willing to do the work for less.

There is a substantial underground economy among apparel contractors. No one knows exactly how many shops operate without licenses or paying taxes, but estimates are that as many as one-third of all apparel factories fall into this sector. Some of the underground operations are small and operate out of people's homes, but some are substantial in size.

The small size and dispersion of apparel contracting firms in Los Angeles also means that they can fairly easily evade state inspection. The number of state inspectors does not remotely come close to the number that would be needed to police the industry systematically. Moreover, even when firms are caught with violations, they can go out of business and open again in a new location, under a new name.

The contracting system enables labor costs to be kept at rock bottom levels. Meanwhile, manufacturers can deny any responsibility for conditions in their contractors' factories because they are "independent" businesses. They can place all the blame for conditions in these shops on the contractors, turning a blind eye to the fact that they set the low prices within which the contractors must operate. The fictional aspect of this claim is evident in the fact that manufacturers often send quality control people to the contractors on a daily basis and keep a tight control over every aspect of production *except* labor standards.

Another way that contracting serves as a labor control system is by inhibiting unionization. The work of a particular manufacturer is spread out over a number of factories. The workers in each of the factories do not even know of each other's existence. Indeed, since manufacturers are very secretive about the identity of their contractors, even the contractors may not know who else works for "their" manufacturers. The dilemma for workers is that, given the low margins in the contracting shops, even if they should win a union struggle, it would be very difficult to get the contractor to pay higher wages. Moreover, the very act of trying to organize a factory is likely to lead the manufacturer to shift production away from that factory, and the workers would be left without jobs.

Workers are more likely to be successful if all those employed by contractors who work for the same manufacturer are able to find common cause. In other words, workers need to organize the entire production system of a single manufacturer simultaneously if they are to have any chance of success. Only then can they demand that the *manufacturer* face the demands for higher wages and benefits, since it is the manufacturer who profits most from their labor and who has accumulated the surplus from which increases could be drawn. But the dispersion of the workforce into multiple, small factories makes coordination extremely difficult. It is in this sense that the contracting system is a well-honed, anti-union device.

The Garment Industry Workforce

Garment workers in Los Angeles are virtually all immigrants. Using the 1990 Census PUMS data, I examined the distribution of apparel industry occupations by the ethnicity of those employed in them (see Table 1).[4] As can be seen, close to 80% of the workers fall into the blue collar occupations of crafts, operatives, and laborers. Focusing on the operatives, the category closest to "garment workers," namely, sewing machine operators, we find that 52% are Mexican, 16% are Central American, and 7% are other Latinos, adding up to about three-fourths of the entire operative workforce. Asian workers make up another 13%, and the remainder is diverse.

Note that Latinos, especially Mexicans and Central Americans, are overrepresented among the operatives relative to their total presence in the industry. Meanwhile, Europeans, and to a lesser extent, Asians, are overrepresented in the managerial and professional strata of the industry.

Compounding the racial/ethnic division of labor in this industry is the gender division of labor. Two-thirds of total industry employees are female, while one-third are male. However only 50% of those males are employed as operatives, in contrast to 72% of the females. Put another way, about three-fourths of LA's garment workers are women.

No one knows exactly how many of LA's garment workers lack legal residency papers. Undocumented immigrants are obviously especially vulnerable to exploitation, and their vul-

Table 1. Ethnic distribution of occupations in the LA apparel industry, 1990 (percentages)

Ethnicity	Management	Professional	Sales	Clerical	Craft	Operations	Labor	Total
European	29.4	42.4	43.5	15.9	10.7	2.1	7.3	8.5
African	3.0	3.0	3.2	4.1	2.3	1.1	2.0	1.7
Chinese	10.7	9.1	1.1	4.3	5.6	7.7	4.4	7.1
Korean	15.5	3.0	3.8	3.8	2.8	2.9	0.8	3.9
Other Asian	5.2	6.8	2.7	5.0	3.0	2.5	4.4	3.1
Mexican	15.9	15.9	21.1	39.4	49.7	52.4	51.6	46.5
Central American	4.8	2.3	4.3	10.6	10.9	16.4	45.3	13.7
Other Latin American	4.8	3.0	3.3	5.4	5.4	6.6	6.5	6.0
Other	10.7	14.3	16.8	11.4	9.8	8.4	7.7	9.3
Total	7.6	2.3	3.2	8.0	9.8	64.8	4.3	100.0
(N)	439	132	184	464	569	3755	248	5791

nerability is exacerbated in times of public, anti-immigrant fervor. Not only do they not have any of the usual legal recourse of citizens and permanent residents, but they are threatened with the possibility of exposure and deportation. Employers can use the fear this engenders to full effect. Workers can be intimidated into silence under a burden of oppression. Some garment workers are legal immigrants, but they rarely have the time to learn English and attain citizenship, so they remain without a vote or voice. According to the Census sample, among the Mexicans employed in the apparel industry, 80% are non-citizens. The figure is even higher for Central Americans, with 88% non-citizens.

Conditions in the Shops
There is some variation in the conditions in the garment contracting shops of Los Angeles, but overall conditions are remarkably similar. Garment workers typically work on piece rate, i.e. they are paid for each procedure they complete. This is similar to the pay system in agriculture, where farm workers are paid for the number of pounds they pick.

Both California and federal law require that workers be paid minimum wage and overtime even if they are paid piece rate. The employer needs to keep time cards and ensure that the hourly minimum wage is covered, and that, when employees work over eight hours a day (the law in California until recently), or 40 hours a week (federal and state law), they must be paid 1.5 times their base wage. These regulations are *routinely* violated. Contractors want to pay only the flat piece rate, and they devise every trick in the book to hide the fact that that is what they are doing. They falsify the records, they maintain double books, they use double time cards, they cook up schemes so that overtime is calculated after the fact, they clock workers out after eight hours and pay them in cash thereafter, they have them work off the books on Saturdays, they encourage off-the-books work at home, they get workers to kick back excess earnings in cash, and so forth. Thus, minimum wage and overtime violations are extremely common in this industry. Even when workers are paid the legal minimum, garment workers remain among the lowest-paid workers in Los Angeles, and make up an important segment of the working poor. Using the 1990 Census sample, we estimated that Mexican female apparel industry operatives earned a median of $6500 per year, well below the minimum wage at the time of $8840 for a full-time, year-round worker.

A baseline survey of 69 California garment firms was conducted in 1994 by California and federal labor enforcement agencies. They found that 61% of Southern California firms failed to pay minimum wage and 78% failed to pay overtime. In addition, 74% had record-keeping violations and 41% paid workers in cash.[5] While subsequent surveys have found some diminution in some of these statistics, other areas show an increase in violations. The fact is, violations of the law remain at an excessively high level.

The piecework system encourages self-exploitation, as workers work very fast and for as many hours as possible in order to make a living. It creates the illusion that the worker controls her earnings by her own skill level, and makes it difficult for workers to feel a sense of common exploitation. The illusion of control is occasionally shattered, when workers are shifted to new tasks and find that their earning levels collapse, or when the contractor lowers the piece rate in a cost-cutting move. These kinds of actions are likely to trigger wildcat reactions on the part of workers, who feel that the rug has been pulled out from under them.

Home work is a fairly common feature in the LA apparel industry. Some workers are full-time home workers, while others take work home after hours. While home work may sometimes be attractive to women workers, who combine work with childcare, it is typically associated with the lowest pay when all the worker's costs are added in.[6] None of the usual protections of minimum wage and overtime pay can be ensured because of the underground character of the work.

Garment workers rarely receive any fringe benefits whatsoever. They are typically not given paid vacations or paid sick leave. Medical insurance is virtually non-existent for the worker herself, and out of the question for her family. In other words, the system is geared toward paying workers their piece rate, and that is that. Note that, by not paying for the health care coverage of the workers in his contracting shops, the manufacturer, who can own a very profitable enterprise and be very rich himself, forces his workers to rely on the impoverished LA County health care system. Once again, the contracting system, by creating a false distance between the employer and his workers, enables the manufacturer to avoid taking responsibility and forces the tax payers to pick up what should rightfully be a tab that he pays.

Apart from poverty level wages, garment workers are also subject to other forms of abuse. Since garment contracting shops are small businesses, they lack bureaucratic rules and are subject to the direct authority of the owner and supervisors. This authority can easily be conducted in an arbitrary fashion, with favoritism and discrimination. Workers who are not favored can be given older, less efficient machines, or can be denied work. They can also be subjected to personal abuse of all kinds, from being yelled at to facing sexual harassment. Workers will sometimes say that they can bear the harsh burden of low wages, but cannot endure being treated in an insulting and demeaning manner.

In addition, many garment factories in Los Angeles have serious health and safety violations. In a recent sweep it was found that 96% of factories violated the law, and 72% had such serious violations that they could result in injury or death.[7] The violations included such matters as blocked fire exits, exposed wires, and machines without safety guards. Many of the garment shops of LA could turn into death traps in the event of a fire.

The Return of Sweatshops

We are in an era in which many government officials and others speak of a return of the sweatshop.[8] In the US, garment industry sweatshops were more or less eradicated by a combination of the development of powerful garment worker unions and the

New Deal, which provided support for basic labor standards. Since the 1970s, and especially during the 1980s and 1990s, we have seen an erosion of wages and working conditions in the US apparel industry. In 1950, average weekly wages of US garment workers were 76.5% of the average manufacturing wage. By 1990, this figure had dropped to 54.1%.[9] Despite protests by industry leaders that only a few rotten apples run sweatshops, the reality is that problems are rampant throughout the LA industry.

Why are we seeing the return of sweatshops now? There are many reasons. Globalization certainly plays a critical role. Since apparel manufacturers and retailers can move, or threaten to move offshore, they force local workers to face the grim choice of accepting the jobs as they are, or losing the jobs altogether. Manufacturers and retailers can argue that they can get the work done offshore for a fraction of the price that they can get it done in Los Angeles. So any improvement in wages and working conditions is interpreted as a threat to the continuation of the industry in LA.

It is important to note that there are reasons why the industry has continued to grow in Los Angeles and has not all flown to cheaper labor sites. To a large extent, the LA industry specializes in fashionable clothing, where speed of production is more important than price. Moreover, the lot sizes are small, making them unsuitable for shipping offshore to large assembly plants that specialize in mass production. The small contracting factories of LA are uniquely suited to this kind of specialized production. Apart from that, there are agglomeration effects, where a manufacturer can meet all his production needs right in the vicinity.

While labor costs are clearly a factor in the decision to move offshore, the fact is that labor is only a relatively small percentage of the cost of apparel production. Especially in the realm of fashion and established brand names, what is being sold is more an "image" than the garment *per se*. Firms of this type spend millions of dollars on advertising, including celebrity endorsements, in order to create demand for a product that was relatively cheap to produce. Los Angeles is a city that specializes in image creation, and so does its apparel industry. Rising labor costs are thus only one consideration in the decision to shift production.

This is not to say that the industry might not pack up and move to Mexico should the price of labor rise substantially. It may. Mexico is nearby, and Mexican firms may develop the capacity to engage in LA-style contracting. For the moment, they do not have this capacity so, despite a lot of bluster about leaving whenever a demand is placed on the industry to clean up its act, apparel production still continues to grow in Los Angeles.

Globalization itself can be seen as part of a larger set of trends that have led to the return of sweatshops. These include: the decline of the welfare state and the attack on the labor movement. In general, we have been witnessing an effort on the part of big business to enhance its power and to undermine the power of labor. Workers in the United States (and in other industrial nations) have gradually been stripped of the protections they were able to win in the post-World War II era. Various public programs and social assistance have eroded, unemployment has risen, and real wages have fallen. Meanwhile, business owners, along with the managers and professionals whom they employ, have grown richer and richer. The gap between rich and poor has grown wider. Los Angeles shows these trends even more starkly than the US as a whole.

The first blast of attack against the labor movement occurred when Ronald Reagan became president and broke the Air Traffic Controllers strike. Since then, unions have faced the erosion of the legal environment that had been developed to protect workers' rights to organize during the New Deal. Unfair labor practices on the part of employers have become more flagrant as they have learned that the cost of union busting is minor compared to the cost of having to negotiate a union contract.

Another aspect in the growth of garment sweatshops has been the consolidation of retailing. Since the mid-1980s there has been a major merger movement in retailing, where giant retailers have bought each other out, assuming huge debt in the process. Some retailers have gone bankrupt. Others have become billion dollar giants who can exercise tremendous power over the industry. The United States has far too many stores per consumer, resulting in vicious competition. The retailers now have the power to pressure manufacturers to cut costs, change styles more rapidly, and maintain more inventory.[10] Many retailers themselves now have their own private (or store) label, where they employ their own contractors directly, bypassing the manufacturers altogether. They undercut the major brands, putting price pressure on them. All of this puts pressure down the line of the garment food chain, and the people most impacted by it are the workers, both in the US and elsewhere.

Note that, although firms claim they must cut costs to remain competitive, the cost-cutting knife is rarely applied to the owners, managers, and professionals in the industry. Executive salaries, advertising costs, profits, and similar rewards that go to the non-labor part of apparel production are allowed to soar with no outcry that these costs must be kept in check. The largest apparel manufacturers in Los Angeles are multimillionaires. For example, six of the 100 highest paid executives in Los Angeles are in the apparel industry, and five of them work for one company: Guess? Inc.[11] Maurice Marciano, CEO of Guess, received $3.4 million in salary and bonus in 1996. It is estimated that the three Marciano brothers, who own most of Guess, personally took home close to half a *billion* dollars over the last four years, including salaries, bonuses, distributions to stockholders, and the results of an Initial Public Offering.

The Use of Ethnically Differentiated Middlemen

In Los Angeles, the apparel industry is structured along ethnic lines. The manufacturers are, for the most part, European in origins, though some are Middle Eastern and Asian. Jews play an important role at this level and, while some are immigrants, many are US-born. The contractors, in contrast, are almost all immigrants, as we have stated. They are from all over the world, but the plurality are Asian. Although Koreans are not numerically the most important, they run some of the largest shops and are very visible in the garment district.

The workers, as we have seen, are predominantly Latino immigrants. While there are some Latino contractors, the predominant pattern in the industry is for an Asian contractor to hire Latino workers. There are cases where contractor and workers are of the same ethnicity, and where there are paternalistic linkages between employer and employees. But this is the exception rather than the rule in Los Angeles. In LA, the relationship between contractor and worker tends to be strictly business-like. Exploitation is not softened by familial bonds or the bonds of helping someone from one's homeland.

This pattern of ethnic differentiation between contractors and workers makes Los Angeles different from other US cities, and maybe other garment centers in Europe too. In these places, although garment contractors and workers are also immigrants, they often come from the same country and share certain bonds of obligation. South Asians in Britain employ South Asians. Chinese in New York and San Francisco employ Chinese. And so forth. Obviously, some of this occurs in LA as well. Nor does it prevent exploitation. The infamous Thai "slave shop" of El Monte, uncovered in August 1995, involved Thai contractors employing Thai women workers.

The pattern found in Los Angeles is increasingly found in Mexico and the Caribbean, where Asian entrepreneurs from Korea and Taiwan are coming to countries like Guatemala and the Dominican Republic and hiring local Latino and indigenous workers. These firms serve as contractors for US manufacturers and retailers. This pattern may also be spreading to other US cities, such as New York.

The phenomenon of ethnic difference between the three layers of the industry: manufacturers as white, contractors as Asian, and workers as Latino creates an important dynamic that spills over into the general race relations of the city. Considerable tension is developing between the Asian and Latino communities, since they meet at the front lines of an exploitative system. Meanwhile, the real economic powers, the manufacturers, retailers, real estate owners, bankers, etc., who are mainly native-born whites, do not have to deal with the antagonisms that arise in the workplace, even though they are primarily responsible for them. They can push the blame onto the immigrant entrepreneurs, making them out to be sleazy business operators who mistreat their workers, unlike the good old, decent, American businessman who would never dream of running a sweatshop. Thus is racism fueled, and used to maintain current relations of power and privilege.

Efforts to Eliminate Sweatshops
As the sweatshop scourge has grown, more government attention has been devoted to trying to eliminate it. Both the state of California and the federal government have stepped up enforcement efforts. The dilemma is that catching a contractor often results in that particular firm going out of business, only to open up again in a new location under a different name. Since the manufacturers (and retailers) control the prices that set the conditions under which garment factories operate, the challenge has been to find a method to hold them responsible for what goes on in "their" factories.

The US Department of Labor (DOL) has been especially innovative in trying to untangle this knot. They have used the principle of "hot goods" to force manufacturers to pay attention to the conditions under which their clothes are produced. Hot goods refers to the idea that goods made under illegal conditions cannot be shipped across state borders. In the highly time-sensitive fashion industry, invoking this provision made it imperative for manufacturers to make sure that their contractors could not be found engaging in illegal practices. The DOL was able to get a number of major manufacturers to sign agreements whereby they would undertake to monitor their contractors. These "compliance agreements" have forced the industry to develop compliance programs under which private firms investigate their contractors to make sure that they are obeying the law.

Needless to say, questions get raised about the effectiveness of such an approach. It gets described as "the fox guarding the chicken coop." Even when manufacturers undertake the effort seriously, there are several problems. Workers are afraid to reveal violations for fear they will be fired by the contractor. Contractors are faced with the threat that the work will be taken away from them by the manufacturer, and while this threat may serve as an inducement for some to clean up their act, given the unchanged economics of the situation, for some it just means being more careful in hiding your misdeeds. The truth is, the only real sanction the manufacturer can use against the contractor is the "death sentence"—to stop shipping work, which will probably drive the contractor out of business. Since neither the contractor nor the workers want that, they both "conspire" to hide illegal practices from manufacturer monitors. Moreover, manufacturers themselves may turn a blind eye to problems among their contractors, since they do not want to disturb their production schedules. After all, their prices and practices created the problem in the first place. Their main motivation is to look clean so that the DOL will get off their backs.

New proposals, from the White House Apparel Industry Partnership, for example, suggest the need for independent monitoring both within the US and in the global apparel industry. There is a call to have NGOs and religious groups serve as monitors, so that the problems inherent in self-monitoring are avoided. However, given the years of experience contractors have had in hiding violations, one wonders whether independent organizations will be able to ferret out the problems.

The Heart of the Matter
At the root of the problem lies unequal power. The manufacturers and their allies have power and the workers have none. Not only do apparel manufacturers have all the usual sources of power in relation to their employees, but in this case their relative power is exaggerated by the lack of citizenship rights of the workers. The garment industry in Los Angeles operates in many ways like the old US South, or like the apartheid regime in South

Africa. Workers have no access to state institutions that provide the usual, minimalist protections. As an article in the *Los Angeles Times* stated concerning the recent mayoral election: "L.A.'s mayor is elected by one city to govern another. The Los Angeles that elects the mayor—and other citywide office-holders—remains white and largely affluent; the city the mayor governs is predominantly non-white and largely poor."[12] LA is now 43.5% Latino and 13.8% white, but Latinos make up less than 15% of the electorate.

Let me modify this point a little. LA garment workers do have some legal protections. They are entitled to minimum wage and overtime, and if state agents find that they have been underpaid, they have the right to receive back wages (even if they can rarely be collected). They also have the legal right to unionize (though being undocumented may hinder one's right to reinstatement if one gets fired for union activity). However, they remain highly vulnerable to actions that drastically hurt their interests, from the elimination of an eight-hour-day over-time provision in state law, to the curtailing of social services for their families, to stepped up sweeps by the Immigration and Naturalization Service. In contrast, if they are unhappy with certain policies, major manufacturers can call up the mayor or the governor. The mayor of Los Angeles helped to create an apparel industry organization, known as the California Fashion Association, to protect and promote the industry, on which no representative of labor sits. The workers are voiceless.

The political situation of Latinos in Los Angeles may be changing as more people sign up to become citizens or use the vote to increase the number of Latino political representatives. Nevertheless, immigrant garment workers, especially the undoc-umented, have yet to feel the effects of these changes. Indeed, in April–May of 1998, the Immigration and Naturalization Service (INS) was targeting the LA garment industry for raids and was rounding workers up for possible deportation.[13] There was little that elected officials could do to prevent this.

Unionization is an important answer to the situation faced by Latino garment workers. Workers need to organize and demand that their interests and needs be addressed, regardless of their legal situation in this country. They need to develop grassroots power that forces change. Unfortunately, the garment workers' union is exceedingly weak in LA, with only about 3000 members. This has not always been the case historically, but union membership has eroded in the face of all the forces we have been describing.[14]

Approaches to Unionization
UNITE, the Union of Needletrades, Industrial and Textile Employees, is the main union attempting to help LA garment workers organize themselves. UNITE is a product of the 1995 merger between the International Ladies Garment Workers' Union (ILG) and the Amalgamated Clothing and Textile Workers' Union (ACTWU). UNITE's LA Organizing Department is currently directed by Mauricio Vazquez, and the organizers are all Latino, the majority of whom have arisen from the ranks of garment workers themselves. Their devotion to the organizing task is unswerving, but the industry poses formidable obstacles.

The contracting system severely hampers union organizing efforts, as we have seen. If the workers in a contracting shop get organized, that factory will be boycotted by the manufacturers and will be driven out of business. Organizing in this industry thus requires special strategies. In particular, you need to bind the manufacturer into the union contract so that he pays enough to the contractors to cover union level wages and benefits. He must be made to work only or predominantly with union shops that guarantee those wages and benefits. A union contract of this sort, known as a Jobber's Agreement, is the only form of "joint liability" that can succeed because it is guarded by the workers themselves.

How does one win such an agreement? In Los Angeles, apparel industry leaders are determined to withstand unionization at all costs. They do not want to concede an inch of their power. Thus, the effort to unionize becomes a war, in which the union must hurt a company severely in order to drive it to negotiate. You practically have to drive the company out of business, and even then, some would rather die than work with a union.

However, the situation is ripe with dialectical possibilities. Every strength has its weaknesses and every weakness has its strengths. Because the contracting system is based on loose ties between manufacturers and contractors, it is vulnerable to the disruption of production flows. For example, other manufacturers who use contractors in the same production system may agree, under pressure, to shift work away from a contractor with whom the union has a labor dispute, leaving the contractor more vulnerable to shutting down. The target manufacturer will have difficulty finding new contractors to work for him, especially in the middle of a labor dispute. In addition, truckers, who play a vital role in transporting goods in a dispersed production system, may support the garment workers by refusing to cross their picket line. In other words, the contracting system has its weaknesses in the face of organizing drives.

Contractors themselves are an interesting group in terms of unionization. On the one hand, it represents instant death for them if they are the only target and they feel compelled to fight against. On the other hand, if the union is able to win a Jobber's Agreement, then they benefit from the higher prices and improved stability of the relationship with the manufacturer. In the long run they have an interest in unionization, but in the short run, they have a deadly opposition to it. However, preliminary agreements can sometimes be negotiated whereby they cooperate with the union in anticipation that the entire production system will be organized.

Apart from attempting to organize one manufacturer and its contractors as a single production system, other approaches are possible. One that is less threatening to a manufacturer is the organizing of an entire sector at one time. In LA much of the industry falls into the amorphous category of "sportswear," but a few distinctive sectors stand out, such as denim, dresses, and swimwear. If enough resources can be mustered, an attempt could be made to organize all the manufacturers and contractors in that sector.

Apart from attempting to hurt a company by interfering in its production flows—a process that can be vital to the time-sensitive apparel industry—unions have learned that companies are vulnerable in the non-production aspects of their operations. Sometimes called corporate campaigns, the idea is to examine all the relationships and plans of the company for their pressure points. These include relationships with financial agents, with distributors and retailers, and with community groups and consumers. In the case of fashion, where image contributes so much to the value of the product, an attack on the image of a company can be very damaging.

One of the advantages of corporate campaigns is that they can follow a company offshore. If an apparel manufacturer flees the accusation that they are using sweatshops in the US, they can equally be accused of exploiting workers in other countries. Since the clothes are still sold by US retailers to US consumers, those consumers can be as outraged about conditions for workers in Vietnam and Guatemala as they are about conditions in Los Angeles. Indeed, some very successful campaigns have been waged against companies who exploit abroad. True, they have generally not been union organizing campaigns, but they have certainly revealed the weaknesses of firms to this kind of negative publicity.

Needless to say, corporate strategies are all adjuncts to worker organizing. Aroused workers cannot win a campaign without having a strategy that is based on a thorough understanding of the industry's dynamics. But on the other hand, a union cannot win such a campaign without worker support and involvement. The two must go hand in hand.

Organizing such vulnerable workers is a difficult task. Some academics romanticize the situation by claiming the immigrants are on the brink of militance. Certainly there have been some noteworthy immigrant worker movements in LA, such as the drywallers' strike, but the immigrant workforce can hardly be described as ready for a general strike—devastating though that would be to the local economy. Latino garment workers are surely aware of their oppression and do sometimes engage in spontaneous protest against egregious actions on the part of their employers. But their poverty and political vulnerability make it very difficult for them to take risks.

For this reason, other types of organizing apart from direct union organizing in a campaign to win a contract have arisen. These include community-based efforts that try to engage in basic worker education and service. UNITE, for example, has worked with the idea of a Garment Workers' Justice Center that encourages participation by garment workers no matter what labels they are sewing. At the time of writing, an effort is being made to work with Catholic Church parishes known to have large numbers of garment workers among their congregants. Much more could be done to lay the basic groundwork for more militant struggles. Even so, being prepared to fight back is not enough. The challenge is to learn not only how to fight, but how to *win*.

The Guess Campaign
UNITE is currently engaged in an effort to organize the largest LA garment manufacturer, Guess? Inc. Guess is a company that has sales of over $500 million per year. It is a highly profitable company that can certainly afford to pay its workers a living wage. The company is super anti-union and has used every trick in the book to try to break the union, from firing union sympathizers, to organizing anti-union demonstrations, to litigating every point it can. If the Marcianos only spent a fraction of what they pay for their high-priced lawyers, public relations firms, and union-busting consultants on supplementing workers' wages, the workers in their contracting shops would make a living wage. Needless to say, their anti-union activism receives strong endorsement from the rest of the industry, which fears the opening of a door that would transform the power relations in the industry for them all.

So far the union campaign has involved multiple tactics. Apart from organizing workers both in Guess's inside shop, where they employ cutting and warehouse workers, and in their contracting shops, the union has been able to show that violations, including illegal home work, are rampant in Guess's contracting network. Guess was the first apparel firm to sign a self-monitoring compliance agreement with the DOL, and it is clear that they have not been able to eliminate sweatshops from their own production network. The union has also put pressure on Guess's own retail stores, consisting of boutiques in upscale malls where private property rights protect stores against social protest. And it is building a major campaign against the department stores that carry Guess clothes.

Of course, there are those who argue that unionization will push the industry more quickly to move all of its production to Mexico. Guess has already moved some of its production there, though its management denies that this has anything to do with union organizing. No doubt some movement south would result if garment workers became organized, although it seems likely that certain sectors will remain, at least for a while. Besides, the cost pressure from organized workers may drive some manufacturers to seek new technologies and labor systems that are less dependent on sweated labor. These technologies and labor systems are being experimented with in the US south, where a labor shortage is driving up wages to some degree. Finally, the movement of at least parts of the industry south may compel UNITE to develop a full-fledged cross-border organizing effort, to the benefit of workers on both sides of the border.

Conclusion
The rising political power of the Latino community in Los Angeles may ultimately be able to change the environment for Latino immigrant garment workers, but this will be a slow and indirect process. In the meantime, workers must take their fate into their own hands and develop direct power through organization. The challenge of unionizing this industry is formidable, but, with the help of community supporters, the workers will prevail.

Notes
1. See Edna Bonacich *et al., Global Production: The Apparel Industry in the Pacific Rim* (Philadelphia: Temple University Press, 1994); Kitty Dickerson, *Textiles and Apparel in the Global Economy*, 2nd ed. (Englewood Cliffs, NJ: Prentice Hall, 1995); Gary Gereffi and Miguel

Korzeniewicz (eds.), *Commodity Chains and Global Capitalism* (Westport, CT: Praeger, 1994); Ian M. Taplin and Jonathan Winterton (eds.), *Rethinking Global Production: A Comparative Analysis of Restructuring in the Clothing Industry* (Brookfield, VT: Ashgate, 1997).

2. American Apparel Manufacturers Association (AAMA), *Focus: An Economic Profile of the Apparel Industry* (Arlington: AAMA, 1996), p. 4.

3. Jack Kyser, *Manufacturing in Los Angeles* (Los Angeles: Economic Development Corporation, 1997), p. 4.

4. PUMS stands for Public Use Microdata Samples, a 5% sample drawn from the 1990 Census that was asked far more detailed questions than the public at large.

5. Targeting Industries Partnership Program (TIPP), *Fourth Annual Report* (Sacramento: TIPP, 1996), p. 18.

6. Rosa Maria Fregoso, *The Invisible Workforce: Immigrant Home Workers in the Garment Industry of Los Angeles,* MA thesis in Latin American Studies (Berkeley: University of California, 1988).

7. TIPP, *op. cit.,* p. 18.

8. Andrew Ross (ed.), *No Sweat: Fashion, Free Trade, and the Rights of Garment Workers* (London: Verso, 1997).

9. AAMA, *op. cit.,* pp. 19–20.

10. Laura Bird and Wendy Bounds, "Stores' Demands Squeeze Apparel Companies," *Wall Street Journal* (July 15, 1997), p. B1.

11. Ben Sullivan, "Bankers, Financiers Dominate Ranks of LA's Highest Paid," *Los Angeles Business Journal* (June 23, 1997), p. 1.

12. Tim Rutten and Peter Y. Hong, "For Candidates, Race Relations a Complex Issue," *LA Times* (March 30, 1997), p. A1.

13. Kristi Ellis, "INS 'Operation Buttonhole' Sweep Collars 75 Undocumented Workers," *Women's Wear Daily* (April 29, 1998), p. 13.

14. John Laslett and Mary Tyler, *The ILGWU in Los Angeles 1907–1988* (Inglewood, CA: Ten Star Press, 1989).

Martha E. Gimenez
University of Colorado at Boulder

Latino Politics—Class Struggles: Reflections on the Future of Latino Politics

Abstract *This paper is a set of reflections about the future of Latino politics in the United States. All politics built around an identity presuppose the reality of that identity. In this paper, I examine the structural and ideological barriers to Latino identity formation and the structural commonalities that shape the experiences conducive to Latino identity formation. After I outline the major divisions in the "Hispanic"/Latino population, I present a theoretical analysis of identity formation and the functions of identity politics, theorizing the ways in which the characteristics of this population foster or hinder the development of Latino identity. The main argument of this paper is that preferences for and debates about ethnic labels/identities and ethnic claims often mask class divisions and class-based grievances within this population and that recognition of the relationship between class location, identity formation, and identity politics might be a necessary step for the development of successful Latino workers' politics.*

Introduction

This paper is, as its subtitle indicates, a set of reflections on the future of Latino politics in the US. The existence of Latino politics is predicated on the existence of Latino identity, and it is the problematic nature of the latter that raises questions about the viability of the former as a future strong component of US politics.

As we approach the end of the 20th century, demographers, social scientists, politicians, and the media speculate about the future racial and ethnic composition of the US population, with the goal of assessing its potential economic, social,

0739–3148/98/040475–10 © 1998 Caucus for a New Political Science

and political implications, such as, for example, changes in the meaning of national identity, the balance of power between Democrats and Republicans, the probability of racial/ethnic conflicts, labor force size and ethnic composition, etc. Paramount among these concerns is awareness of the "Hispanic"/Latino population's potential for growth as a result of natural increase and immigration from Latin America. As projections indicate, "Hispanics"/Latinos will become the largest ethnic minority population in the US.[1]

The idea that "Hispanics"/Latinos could vastly surpass African Americans in both numbers and political influence might be worrisome to all of the following: those who perceive the growth of racial/ethnic minority populations as a threat to racial purity and the "majority" status of "whites"; those concerned with the downsizing of the welfare state while future demand for its resources is likely to grow; those who cannot fathom the possibility of trans-racial/ethnic solidarity and forecast escalating conflicts between "Hispanics"/Latinos and other minorities; and, in general, those who see the effects of immigration as a threat to some mythical national identity, rather than as one of several processes which continuously undermine and simultaneously rebuild national identity as an expression of historical continuity and change. On the other hand, a high rate of growth might be a matter of rejoicing for "Hispanic"/Latino politicians, for whom larger potential constituencies mean a more solid basis for their political careers and greater leverage with state and federal bureaucracies and legislative bodies.

Both negative views (i.e. those focused on fears of intensified racial/ethnic conflicts around scarce resources and jobs, the effects of intermarriage, or threats to national identity) and positive views (i.e. those who value cultural diversity or expect political gains) assume that this growing population can and will be politically mobilized, thus becoming a political force to be reckoned with. Is that a realistic understanding of this phenomenon? I think not. Perhaps the most important barrier to the equation of size with political strength is the ambiguity inherent in the difficulties of naming this population, an ambiguity that reflects its heterogeneous nature. Although this paper is about Latino politics, I began with some considerations about the "Hispanic"/Latino population to highlight the elusive nature of Latino identity, even though to speak of Latino politics presupposes the existence of a Latino identity as its foundation. It will be my argument in this paper that the possibility of Latino politics may be affected both negatively and positively by the heterogeneous nature and, consequently, the problematic identity of the population which is its material base. After I briefly outline the major divisions in the "Hispanic"/Latino population, I will present some ideas about identity formation and the functions of identity politics, theorizing the ways in which the characteristics of this population may foster or hinder the development of an all-encompassing ethnic identity. I will argue that preference for and debates about ethnic labels/identities and ethnic claims often mask class divisions and class-based grievances within this population and that recognition of the relationship between class location and identity politics might be a necessary step for the development of successful Latino politics.

Identity Politics/Labeling Politics: Unraveling the "Hispanic" Label

The legal definitions currently used to classify individuals as members of racial and ethnic minorities do not apply exclusively to members of social groups historically oppressed in the US. They apply to heterogeneous populations constructed on the basis of racial/ethnic definitions used by the Bureau of the Census and continuously reproduced by private and public sources of data gathering and dissemination. The population variously called "Hispanic" or Latino is no exception. I put the "Hispanic" label between quotation marks to indicate its bureaucratic origins, as the latest Census effort to identify a population which by its very nature defies characterization. This umbrella term includes colonized people of Spanish, Mexican, and Puerto Rican descent who have been in this country for generations, having been incorporated together with their lands after the 19th century wars between the US, Mexico, and Spain. It also includes waves of legal and undocumented immigrants from Cuba, Mexico, Central and South America; businessmen, professional, and skilled workers "pulled" by better opportunities; and political and economic refugees fleeing from political repression and the chronic unemployment and poverty of their countries of origin. In addition to immigration experience in the US, citizenship status and national origin (variables which determine vast cultural differences), this population is divided by class, socioeconomic status, language (not everyone speaks Spanish, and many who do don't speak English), and race/ethnicity. "Hispanic"/Latinos could be of any "race" and many are multiracial, from Native American, European, Asian, or African ancestry.[2]

How can a common identity be forged out of these enormous differences? Under what conditions would individuals so varied in their backgrounds and opportunities somehow overcome their differences to see themselves as part of a larger collectivity? An important barrier to the formation of a transnational/trans-cultural Latino identity is the unique American meaning of the umbrella labels; they reflect compromises within the US political scene and are incomprehensible to visitors and newly arrived immigrants from Latin America and Spain. This is why many reject it, while some may adopt it for purely instrumental reasons, if it will give them access to social, economic, or political resources. Given that "Hispanic" refers to anything pertaining to Spain (the former colonizer), to many Latin Americans (like myself) it is a politically distasteful label, yielding nothing but a bogus identity that blurs the qualitative differences between Latin Americans, Spaniards, and people of Spanish, Mexican, Cuban, and Puerto Rican descent who have lived in the US for generations. True, every national origin label (e.g. Latin American, Spanish, etc.) erases class, socioeconomic status, racial, ethnic, and other important social divisions but, when compared to a newly politically constructed label, such as "Hispanic," they are qualitatively different in their meaning for the populations which claim them, for in their eyes these labels appear as "natural," as "who they really are." But, more importantly, they signal important differences among the actual experiences and culture of people. Ultimately, from a Marxist theoretical standpoint, differences in national origin, culture, race, ethnicity, etc., tend to be minimized by common class location so that, for example, middle and upper class immigrants from Latin America are likely to have more in common with US people of similar class standing than with working class or poor Latinos.

Furthermore, within the US, "Hispanic" and Latino have negative class and cultural connotations because they denote a population with which the media, social scientists, and the average person associate a variety of negative social patterns (e.g. female headed households, high school dropouts, welfare recipients, gangs, delinquent behavior, etc.) caused, presumably, by its racial/cultural characteristics. The uses of the "Hispanic" label, frequently in the context of data describing racial differences, encourage the false assumption that it refers to a race (e.g. "Hispanics" are included within the "people of color" category), though the fine print accompanying the data points out that they could be of any race. The proportion of Central and South American immigrants from mixed or pure Native American, African, Asian, or European descent varies according to country of origin, with Southern Cone countries having the larger proportion of citizens of European descent. This complex mixture of ancestries produces interesting contradictory implications: "Hispanics" of Native American descent are made invisible by the term's pseudo-European veneer while everyone, at the same time and regardless of ancestry, is presumed to be "non-white" unless proven otherwise. It is these class, pseudoracial, and pseudocultural implications of the label that make it so pernicious, as a source of damaging stereotypes that affect the interaction between whites and members of this population. This is why middle and upper class individuals may refuse to adopt these forms of panethnic or transnational identities, unless, of course, they find that it is in their benefit to do so for specific purposes, such as, for example, claiming minority status to benefit from Affirmative Action or from government contracts.

While these drawbacks to the label may seem obvious, especially to foreigners, they are outweighed, in the eyes of many, by the perceived advantages of being able to identify and estimate the size of this population, and claim benefits and protection from the state. This label, "Hispanic," is not a product of bureaucratic fiat but of the congruence between bureaucratic need for better identification and counting and social scientists' and politicians' demand for better population estimates. It is here that the harmony between the political, social, economic, and administrative status quo and the politics of identity become self-evident.

Unlike most countries, where the existence of classes and class struggles is acknowledged in common sense and legitimate political discourse, the US is silent about class and obsessed with racial/ethnic politics, although age and gender also occupy a prominent place. This situation is the result of the complex interaction of many factors: the heritage of slavery, the presence of colonized minorities, past and current immigration, the lasting political effects of McCarthyism, and the ongoing unraveling of the capital–labor contract established after World War II. Last, but not least, current and future changes in the composition of the US population and in the opportunities opened to its citizens are the outcome of world capitalist processes. The US, like all advanced capitalist countries, is experiencing processes of social dislocation and economic disruption similar to those inflicted for so long on the rest of the world. Local capital flight, foreign capital moving in, speculation, deindustrialization, flexibilization of labor contracts, growth in temporary employment, decline in real wages, etc., signal the end of the privileges of labor aristocracies and the return to heightened competition for economic survival.

It is within this context that we have to place the development of the politics of identity and the conflation of class struggles with civil rights struggles. The processes of capitalist development which allowed for the structural, social, and cultural integration of European immigrants prior to World War II also excluded and marginalized large sectors of the population,

especially those defined as "non-white." The racialization, ethni-
cization, and genderization of sectors of the labor force coincide
with their relegation to the lowest ranks of the occupational
structure or to semi-proletarianized and excluded sectors of the
reserve army of labor. The political construction of the
"Hispanic" label is one response to the need to find political
strength in numbers in a context where class grounds for political mobilization are precluded and the only viable acceptable
form of articulating grievances and political mobilization for
racial/ethnic minorities is through the acceptance and perhaps
internalization of the racial/ethnic identities the larger society
imposes upon them.

The "Hispanic" label is, however, primarily a response
from above, from the state and from elite individuals concerned
not just with the amelioration of the conditions affecting their
communities but with building the basis for their own political
advancement at the local, state, and even national levels. The
political construction of Latino identity, on the other hand, is
the grassroots response to the need for political mobilization
from below, through a form of self-identification likely to make
more sense even to the foreign-born, constructed in terms of
the historical heritage of the diverse populations willing to
embrace that term and make it their own.

Identity is a subjective phenomenon, a product of people's
choice, a form of self-awareness that helps people make sense of
their experiences and understand who they are. It is useful to
differentiate between "legitimation identities," which are the
creation of the dominant institutions to strengthen their domination over subordinate groups, and "resistance identities,"
which are the creation of social actors located in the most deval-
ued and stigmatized positions.[3] In the present US context, however, resistance identities have also legitimizing functions in so
far as they replace class awareness and limit themselves to struggles which, even when victorious, leave the structural source of
grievances unchanged.

But before pursuing this line of thought, it is important to
theorize the process of identity formation and explore the con-

ditions that would lead individuals to be receptive to "Hispanic" or to Latino identities. To the barriers to the emergence of a transnational or panethnic identity inherent in the heterogeneity of the "Hispanic" population must be added the effects of current changes in the US economy that increase economic competition in a political climate characterized by powerful anti-immigrant and racist ideologies. The recent challenges to Affirmative Action and all state policies and laws designed to redress the effects of past discriminations reflect not only white racism but the overall economic uncertainty that affects most US workers, white and non-white, and illustrate the extent to which political and economic conflicts are fought under racial banners, thus making the adoption of a racial/ethnic identity a matter of survival rather than a lifestyle option.

Althusser's views on ideology are useful to unravel the processes of racial/ethnic ideological constructions and the limitations of identity politics.[4] Ideologies have a material existence; they exist in an apparatus and its practices and in the practices they elicit from those who live in the truth of the ideology (i.e. uncritically, within its parameters). In the United States, the ideological state apparatus most important in the production of racial/ethnic ideologies is the bureau of the Census which, together with federal, state, and other institutions, produce and reproduce "racial"/"ethnic" identities through the classification of people, gathering of data, and dissemination of information. In turn, these labeling practices go on in countless other public and private institutional settings (e.g. the army, schools, hospitals, etc.). Identities also emerge from the grassroots, as effects of macro level historical processes and struggles and ongoing processes of economic exclusion, economic exploitation, political resistance, and civil rights struggles. At the confluence of top down and grassroots determinants of racial/ethnic identity formation is the existence of population aggregates excluded (in varying degrees) from full political and social integration, relegated to the lower echelons of the occupational structure and condemned to disproportionately high rates of unemployment, underemployment, and welfare dependency. While the focus of this essay is the population aggregate composed of Mexican Americans, Puerto Ricans, Cubans, and Latin Americans, this discussion of identity formation has broader implications. Racist ideologies legitimate these exclusions on "racial," "ethnic," or "cultural" grounds. Exclusions are conducive to the maintenance and reproduction over time of patterns of behavior, including language, that become the material basis for identity formation and for the effectivity of the legitimating ideologies. This is the terrain for the material practices and rituals (e.g. dances, music, religious and patriotic holidays, family traditions, etc.) which individuals freely reproduce, acting according to their belief in who they are.

State sponsored and grassroots identities have similar ideological effects despite their often dissimilar political goals. The crucial function of ideology is to constitute concrete individuals as subjects; "Ideology interpellates individuals as subjects... there is no ideology except by the subject and for subjects."[5] Identity politics is the politics of subjects par excellence. Ideologies of racial/ethnic and other politically constructed identities (e.g. gender, age, sexual preference, etc.) interpellate concrete individuals as subjects, as who they always already are, for the interpellation often begins to operate before birth.[6] For example, identities reflecting national origin or ancestry (e.g. Mexican American, Puerto Rican, Colombian, Spanish, etc.) operate from birth, so that individuals "naturally" see themselves as Puerto Ricans, Cubans, etc. Social movements and state intervention can result in the construction of new identities (e.g. Chicano, Latino, "Hispanic," African American, senior citizen, etc.), but these also trigger the experience of recognition, as if the interpellation had the power to make the pieces of individuals' lives suddenly fit into a pattern that is objectively new from the standpoint of the observer (i.e. politically constructed, the effect of macro level processes that cannot be reduced to the subject's agency or intentionality) but seems at the same time to have been always already there, as a primordial aspect of the subject's identity. Using a pop-psychology expression, ideological interpellation generates, most of the time, the "aha" experience of recognizing the obvious, that which is and has always been the case.

However, it is only under certain historical conditions that people whose initial identities reflect national origin and ancestry come to see themselves in terms of current racial/ethnic identities. It cannot be assumed that ethnic/racial ideologies and labels, whether grassroots or state sponsored, should always succeed in creating racial/ethnic subjects. Althusser is probably right in arguing that the function of ideology is to constitute concrete individuals as subjects through processes of interpellation and recognition. But he seems to assume that all interpellations are successful, leaving no room for challenge and resistance. Early interpellations during the formative years are indeed successful; but, depending on historically changing conditions, adults are capable of resisting the ideological pressure to become that which the ideology and the purveyors of ideology tell them that they really are.

The theoretically and politically important issue that arises at this point is that of the identification of the material conditions (objective and subjective) necessary for the success or failure of ideological interpellations in the construction of racial/ethnic identities. Just as people make history under circumstances not of their own creation,[7] individuals construct themselves as subjects through the combined effects of ideological interpellations and of their material conditions of existence.

Among these conditions, the working class location of the populations that eventually organize themselves as "Hispanics"/Latinos is perhaps the most salient determinant of identity formation in conjunction with the ideological interpellations that surround them from the state, from the media, from the city and state bureaucracies with which they have to deal with, and from the population at large who has also been indoctrinated by the relentless use of umbrella terms that reduce the enormous complexity of the US population to a few generic identities: white, Asian, African American, "Hispanic"/Latino, and Native American.

As Padilla has shown in his study of the development of Latino ethnicity in Chicago, the structural factors that led to the emergence of a Latino ethnicity and identity were the shared inequalities affecting Mexicans and Puerto Ricans in the areas of housing, education, and employment.[8] Populations different in their national origins, culture, citizenship status, language, immigration experience, etc., came together not on the basis of a preexisting common identity as Latinos or "Hispanics," but as people who shared common experiences of discrimination in education and employment, relegated to the worse jobs and forced to live in crowded and unsanitary conditions. Now, these common experiences of economic exploitation and racial discrimination came about because of who they were, not in their own eyes, but in the eyes of US beholders who, depending on the nature of immigration patterns and the history of different cities and states, are likely to refer to everyone as "Mexican," "Hispanics," etc., regardless of the actual national origins, ancestry, class, etc., of the people thus labeled. Other important structural factors contributing to the development of transnational ethnicity, as Padilla indicates, are the federal and state civil rights laws and policies, such as Affirmative Action, designed to redress the effects of past discrimination and stop or at least diminish current discriminatory practices in the areas of employment, education, and business. The law protected "Hispanics" and made them eligible for a variety of benefits, including AFDC, food stamps, Medicaid, and other benefits. Under these conditions, people are put in the position of having to admit to being who the law and others say they are, so that they too can qualify for legal aid and state support.

The development of Latino ethnicity, then, becomes eminently pragmatic, situational (as Padilla convincingly argued), and, consequently, unstable and localized. It cannot be assumed, given that the composition of the "Hispanic"/Latino populations varies by region of the country, states, counties, and cities, that politically organized, self-identified Latinos in New York City, for example, are similar in culture, ancestry, language skills, etc., to Latinos in Los Angeles, Chicago, Denver, or San Francisco. On the other hand, despite those and other differences, they are likely to be similar in class location. The major assumption underlying my argument is that only working class, poor, and near poor members of the population the Census classifies as "Hispanic" are likely to coalesce in community and political organizations, mobilized as Latinos or perhaps "Hispanics," in efforts to deal with state bureaucracies, city governments, school boards, developers, party organizations, etc., in order to seek solutions to common problems such as housing discrimination, educational concerns (e.g. dropout rates, test scores, tracking), jobs, working conditions, etc. Latino consciousness emerges in the context of communities and work places where people experience similar problems; middle, upper–middle, and upper class "Hispanics"/Latinos are unlikely to experience those problems and unlikely to live in ethnic enclaves, unless they happen to own businesses or provide services that employ and/or serve a population of their peers. I am, therefore, arguing that ideological interpellations are likely to be successful in producing "Hispanic"/Latino subjects only in working class communities and work places, in ethnic enclaves where employed, underemployed, unemployed, and poor people live together, experiencing similar economic and social problems. Latino identity, in other words, is not purely a form of racial/ethnic identity but also an expression of class location and a base from which class grievances can be articulated so that they can be heard.

Class location is the basis for both the weakness and the strength of Latino identity and Latino politics. It is, however, easier to perceive the weaknesses than the strengths. It is easier to point out how class and other cleavages within the "Hispanic"/Latino population make it difficult for people to feel that they belong together, thus undermining the possibility of nationally important Latino politics in the future. It is also possible to point out the weakness inherent in situational politics, local, narrow, focused on specific issues, and, paradoxically, a source of problems even as it may succeed in attaining short term solutions to specific problems. Identity politics have a dialectics of their own; the maintenance of an identity requires its positing itself as different from other identities, so that a Latino identity makes sense only *vis-à-vis* other racial/ethnic identities. The political terrain then becomes one in which racial/ethnic struggles become endemic and entrenched; in which the successful emergence of racial/ethnic identities to struggle against economic and racial/ethnic discrimination contributes to the maintenance of the racial/ethnic distinctions and antagonisms that generate the problems different racial/ethnic groups would like to solve. This, therefore, raises questions about the extent to which a strong Latino presence in the national political scene would be desirable, to the extent that strong ethnic/racial identities are the source of endemic structural conflicts and struggles for jobs, housing, and state and local funds and other resources.

But also inherent in the very nature of Latino identity are the sources of its potential strength and positive contribution to national politics. As I argued above, Latino identity emerges in a working class setting and in the process of workers articulating working class concerns affecting their working conditions, their families, and the future of their children. If Latino politics, presumably representing the interests of all Latinos, regardless of class, were to become, instead, Latino workers' politics, making public its structural base while the identity is broadened to embrace both its cultural, racial/ethnic and its class-based concerns, it could become a bridge for workers to come together regardless of racial/ethnic differences. This would entail recognition, among Latino political leaders, of the political significance of the class differences among Latinos and of the common interests between Latino and non-Latino working class people. It would be a momentous change in American politics if Latinos were to start bringing back class to the repertoire of acceptable political discourse, by crafting an identity based both on sources of cultural meaning—Latino—as well as on sources of economic hardship and potential economic advancement—as workers who happen to be Latinos.

Conclusion

This short essay presents a theoretical assessment of the possibilities open to Latino politics in the US at the present time. I have stressed the heterogeneity of the population variously called "Hispanic" or "Latino," indicating how the unique role of these umbrella labels conspires against their acceptance among the people they are supposed to name, especially among the foreign-born. I have also depicted these labels as forms of ideological interpellation which, under certain material conditions, are likely to produce "Hispanic" or Latino subjects. I argued that the conditions favorable for the emergence of Latino identities, which are the foundation for the development of Latino politics, are working class conditions and that, in that sense, it is through identity politics that Latinos can voice their grievances and organize to protect their interests. But given that those grievances stem not only from racial discrimination but also from economic exploitation and are, fundamentally, also working class grievances, I have argued that here lies the basis for the potential strength of Latino politics. To the extent Latino politics remains a form of identity politics intent on pursuing gains for the Latino population only, it will unwittingly contribute to the strength and permanence of racial/ethnic divisions, for those divisions rest precisely on the endurance of those identities through time as grounds for never-ending struggles for ever dwindling resources and opportunities. But to the extent Latinos embrace the other important source of their social and economic plight, their class position within the US class structure, and assume their identity as Latino workers, Latino politics can become a spearhead for a resurgence of working class strength through working class politics that pursue not the interests of "generic" workers but of workers proud of both that which makes them special and that which makes them brothers and sisters in struggle.

I am aware of the apparently utopian nature of this view, given the current context of powerful identity politics, seemingly indestructible racism, and growing anti-immigrant politics. But based on my understanding of the basis for the potential strength of political actors in capitalist societies, I believe that as long as Latino politics remains local, situational, and at most regional in nature, it will remain weak, its success linked to some degree to its failure to be more than factional identity politics.

While the benefits these politics may bring to their constituencies are real, the side effects of identity politics is to cement identity-based differences and conflicts. While some middle and upper–middle class Latino politicians may build their political careers on the basis of clinging on to a purely racial/ethnic base, it is not clear that their interests and the interests of their working class constituencies may coincide in the long run. To the extent Latino political and union leaders emerge who are not afraid of challenging the political wisdom of adhering to a purely racial/ethnic identity and understand the potential strengths and advantages that result from acknowledging the largely working class nature of Latino grievances and problems, Latino workers might emerge as an important new presence in the national political scene.

The forces of the global economy which are beginning to break the nationalist barriers among workers from different nations are intensifying the competition between "majority" and "minority" workers in this country and as long as workers cling to their racial/ethnic identities overlooking their common interests, racism and racial discrimination will thrive. Perhaps it will be the historical role of Latino workers and other so-called minority workers to break the limits of identity politics by reclaiming all the determinants of their identities; not just their culture, their language, their historical heritage, and their current selective understandings of their traditions and sense of who they are, but also their class location and their understanding of themselves as workers who with their labor and the labor of their ancestors and the future labor of their children are making this nation what it is. The future of Latino politics is in the hands of Latino workers; the future of American politics could change if Latino politics were to become Latino workers' politics.

Notes

1. I place "Hispanic" between quotation marks to highlight its politically constructed nature from above, whereas Latino is a term congruent with the Latin American origins of a large proportion of the population officially classified as "Hispanic."

2. Martha E. Gimenez, "Latino/'Hispanic': Why Needs a Name? The Case Against a Standardized Terminology," *International Journal of Health Services* 19:3 (1989), pp. 557–571.

3. Manuel Castells, *The Power of Identity* (London: Blackwell Publishers, 1997).

4. Louis Althusser, *Lenin and Philosophy and Other Essays* (New York: Monthly Review Press, 1971).

5. *Ibid.*, p. 170.

6. *Ibid.*

7. Karl Marx, *The Eighteenth Brumaire of Louis Bonaparte* (New York: International Publishers, [1852] 1969).

8. Felix M. Padilla, *Latino Ethnic Consciousness: The Case of Mexican Americans and Puerto Ricans in Chicago* (Notre Dame, IN: University of Notre Dame Press, 1985).

Richard Santillan
California State Polytechnic University

The Cloning of La Raza Unida Party for the Twenty-first Century: Electoral Pragmatism or Misguided Nostalgia?

Abstract *This article outlines the major contributions of La Raza Unida Party during the height of its popularity. Despite its short political life, La Raza Unida Party made long-lasting contributions to the ongoing struggle for political justice, and its political legacy continues to reverberate in American politics today. This article also explores the numerous reasons for the party's quick demise. The brevity of La Raza Unida Party's presence on the community's political radar screen was due to a combination of external and internal destructive forces that contributed to its inescapable collapse. It is extremely critical to put the spotlight on the party's deficiencies in order for future political movements to sidestep these organizational errors. The conclusion examines the feasibility and wisdom of reviving such a Chicano party within the fast-moving political context of the late 1990s. Is it possible to build a third party for the next millennium based primarily on political expediency and prideful nationalism? Besides addressing this question, the conclusion discusses political and leadership qualities required to lead the community into the next stage of political resurrection. This new leadership must be extremely careful not to give way to the natural impulse of being politically homesick and reverting back to the "good old days" of the Chicano movements in resolving today's electoral uncertainties. Instead, it is critical that this new leadership have a vision of the future based on a clear understanding of the past.*

The 1996 presidential campaign represented a major political setback to the electoral aspirations of Mexican Americans. Unlike previous national presidential campaigns, neither president Bill Clinton nor Republican challenger Robert Dole made convincing efforts to firmly affiliate themselves with this emerging ethnic constituency. Furthermore, both major parties failed to allocate sufficient campaign resources to seriously entice Mexican American voters to support their respective candidates seeking local, state, and congressional offices. Equally alarming was that the Democrats and the Republicans avoided acknowledging and endorsing the specific issues and policies generally supported by the Mexican American community. Instead, both major parties carefully manipulated the issues of immigration, bilingual education, and affirmative action—not in the configuration supported by the Mexican American leadership, but as reactionary wedge issues against the Mexican American community itself.

The unilateral decisions to disregard viable outreach programs clearly signaled the abrupt end of nearly forty years of vague promises to Mexican American voters by both parties. Therefore, the 1996 presidential campaign was not merely a temporary political retreat by the Democrats and Republicans but the stunning termination of nearly four decades of cosmetic competition for the votes of the Mexican American community. Earlier Republican and Democratic "Viva" programs, aimed at wooing Mexican American voters, were token at best, and borderline racist at worst.

This political betrayal is largely due to the fact that both major parties, especially the Democrats, are rapidly moving rightward along the political spectrum by catering to the white middle class. The Democratic Party has come to believe falsely that linking themselves any longer with New Deal "liberal" interest groups is political suicide and therefore has abdicated its political obligation to this historical coalition. Both parties are rapidly becoming disgustingly alike, their political distinctions almost indefinable, as they continue their sinister agreement on bipartisan sweetheart deals at the expense of people of color and the union movement. This Democratic abandonment of Mexican American voters in favor of moderate middle-class voters should not have come as a surprise to the Mexican American leadership in 1996, inasmuch as this electoral opportunism has been gradually and fundamentally shifting over the last few national elections. Thus, the unresolved issues of racism, sexism, homophobia, muticultural and multilingual education, workers' and immigrants' rights, public and mental health, the disparity of wealth between the poor and the rich, and other life-and-death concerns were nearly ignored in 1996. And no doubt things will look even bleaker in 1998 and 2000, when wedge issues will become even more divisive in these upcoming elections.

As a result of this obvious electoral rejection by both major parties, a pessimistic political frame of mind has descended upon the Mexican American community as a whole. The shell-shocked Mexican American leadership finds itself at an electoral impasse, with no place to go with their votes in 1998 and 2000. Many Mexican American leaders are calling for an agonizing reappraisal regarding their shaky political relationship with the Democratic and Republican parties, while other community spokespersons are calling for alternative strategies for future elections. In addition to the political snub by both parties, most Mexican Americans are feeling as though they are under racial and nativist siege, with the current social climate being hysterically anti-immigrant, anti-affirmative action, and antibilingual. All of these negative cross-currents go hand in hand. Reactionary forces now feel empowered to turn back the civil rights clock because progressive Democrats are shirking from their moral obligation in protecting the vital interests of working-class women and men, people of color, and other peripheral groups in society.

The prevailing mood among Mexican Americans is one of political disgust, and many are engaged in trying to find a stop-gap solution to this growing sense of electoral marginalization and ethnic isolationism. As a result of this fortresslike mentality, Mexican American political remedies appear to be both punitive in nature and a defensive ethnic response, including calls for the reestablishment of a Chicano third party—a political flashback to the "golden age" of La Raza Unida Party in the 1960s.

The Formation of La Raza Unida Party
La Raza Unida party did not evolve in political isolation. Its ideological roots and organizational formation were shaped by unprecedented upheaval in politics, culture, and values. La Raza Unida Party was fiercely influenced, for example, by the profound global period swirling around it, including the worldwide antiwar effort, the black civil rights movement, wars of liberation, and the international mobilization of students. La Raza Unida was also the logical extension of two prior ideological stages of Mexican American political development in the twentieth century. With the inclusion of La Raza Unida Party, this historical period has witnessed three significant and interwoven approaches to political integration: assimilation, pluralism, and nationalism. Collectively, all three of these similar outlooks have promoted ballot-box reformism, whereas their unique political identities have been defined by their disagreement regarding the levels of ethnic assimilation necessary for achieving their individual electoral goals. This evolutionary complexity of Mexican American electoral development and its dialectical tug-of-wars regarding the political role of ethnicity eventually led to the emergence of La Raza Unida Party in the 1960s.

While this article will focus solely on the electoral aspects of the community, it is important to point out that there have been other significant Mexican American movements that influenced the birth of La Raza Unida Party, including women's groups, trade unions, religious associations, youth and senior citizens clubs, mutual aid societies, and veteran's organizations. Indeed, the G.I. generation had held political sway in the community from the end of World War II until it found itself staggering into the 1960s and unable to effectively confront the fast-approaching social eruption. By the late 1960s, Mexican Americans from all political persuasions were once again dispirited by both major parties and seeking innovative ways to be key players in the game of politics. The social stage was now set for a new generation of progressive Mexican Americans to fill this political void and to usher in a new political era. The establishment of the Chicano movement quickly shifted the political and cultural gears of the Mexican American community into militant overdrive.

Hence, the Chicano movement was a direct outgrowth of previous political movements within the Mexican American community and the global events whirling around it. The early state of the Chicano movement was quite spontaneous and lacked any clear definition of an ideological mission and political objectives. However, with the ratification of the combined canon of El Plan de La Raza Unida (1967) and El Plan de Aztlan (1969), the political direction of the Chicano struggle became more focused regarding its goals and policies. The Chicano movement combined civil disobedience with an emotional appeal to its Mexican roots.

Thus, from its early, stormy days, the Chicano movement echoed the nationalist sentiments of other international groups calling for their own homeland, since Chicanos did not view themselves as legitimate U.S. citizens. This was not political pie-in-the-sky utopia. Nationalism was viewed as a new line of attack against the scourge of racism. The unconditional demand for a separate Chicano nation was breathtaking in scope and paralleled that, for example, of the Basques in Spain, the French in Canada, the Palestinians in the Middle East, and the Catholics in Northern Ireland. These self-determination movements were gaining strength throughout the world. Moreover, the colonial wars of liberation throughout Latin America, Asia, Africa, and the Middle East intrigued the Chicano leadership by holding out the tangible prospect of its own national sovereignty. The Chicano leadership viewed the Southwest United Sates as occupied land taken illegally by the imperialist war of aggression in 1846 by the United States of North America. As a result, the Chicano movement verbally reclaimed the land and the political freedom that had been taken from their ancestors.

Whereas previous generations of Mexican Americans demanded full U.S. citizenship, the Chicano movement rejected political assimilation and centered its demands on international human rights. Accordingly, the entire Chicano command called for an end to the partition of Aztlan, the legendary homeland of the Aztec people, believed to have originally been located in the southwest portion of North America. Aztlan was viewed as the ultimate political safe haven for the Mexican people. And, in a step similar to those taken by other groups involved in international struggles for nationhood, the Chicano movement established its own distinct political arm—El Partido de La Raza Unida.

The provocative ideology of Chicano nationalism proclaimed by La Raza Unida Party fundamentally consisted of two overlapping principles. First of all, its philosophy was deeply rooted in the belief that all people of Mexican heritage are culturally and historically linked. La Raza Unida Party, for example, emphatically claimed political kinship to the indigenous peoples of pre-Columbian Mexico and with revolutionary Mexican heroes, including Hidalgo, Moreles, Villa, and Zapata. La Raza Unida Party's cultural mantra was that their crusade for political liberation was directly linked to the indigenous ancestry. La Raza Unida Party leaders strongly believed that the Mexican people in the *barrios* of North American were historically bonded by common culture, history, values, attitudes, ambitions, resiliency, and a powerful sense of justice. Thus, La Raza Unida Party designated itself, within this new nation of Aztlan, as the political custodian of the Mexican population, and bravely entered into unchartered political territory.

The second principle was that La Raza Unida Party rejected the political legitimacy and authority of North American politics. It rejected not only the Democratic and Republican parties but also third parties, such as Peace and Freedom and the Socialist Workers Party, because of their Anglo leadership. Unlike previous Mexican American generations, La Raza Unida Party cast aside the liberal vision of ethnic political integration and instead took an oppositional stance against Anglo society. La Raza Unida Party went beyond the reformist politics of the ballot box and appealed instead to a greater global and separatist political agenda. According to La Raza Unida Party activists, the next evolutionary stage after the social failure of ethnic integration was political divorce from the North American electoral system. The La Raza Unida Party secessionist position, inflammatory to some in the community, called for an autonomous Chicano political system with its own self-governing congress, its delegates chosen through the exercise of indigenous democracy among the Mexican masses. The concept of indigenous democracy held that legitimate political power rightfully rested with the Chicano people to create their won political image and base. The leadership of La Raza Unida Party associated unconditional national independence with unrestricted political and cultural freedom. La Raza Unida declared that the Mexican people have the unshared right to develop for themselves their own political destiny and ethnological policies. Obviously, this unabashed radical political declaration of independence challenged not only the two-party system but also the old political order within the Mexican American community as well.

The initial rumblings and first success of La Raza Unida Party took place in south Texas in the late 1960s. This part of the country has been a bastion of political ferment and resistance among Mexican Americans for generations. While struggling tenaciously against racism, La Raza Unida Party leaders established a solid community foundation deeply rooted in mutual self-reliance, family life, cultural preeminence, and political empowerment. La Raza Unida Party was viewed as a political longshot because of the numerous legal challenges to it and the the race and Red-baiting tactics used by the elite Anglo power structure. Yet, in a stunning electoral upset, La Raza Unida candidates captured city council and school board seats in several localities and savored their victories in defiant joy. The electoral triumph of La Raza Unida Party in south Texas immediately had profound implications for the overall Chicano movement because it appeared that the first concrete steps toward nationhood had firmly taken hold. No longer was the rallying cry "Chicano power" merely an abstract slogan for La Raza Unida Party—it was now about indisputable evidence at the grassroots level that a dignified future was possible. La Raza Unida Party's electoral epicenter was south Texas, and it sent political shock waves throughout the rest of the rural and urban *barrios* of

North America. Chicanos from other parts of the nation made pilgrimages to south Texas to witness and celebrate these political victories. For the moment, Crystal City, Texas, was the political mecca of Aztlan.

This new political wind sweeping across the *barrios* of South Texas was viewed as newsworthy by mainstream media and reported throughout the country. Chicano publications also covered the ground-zero activities of La Raza Unida in Texas with joyous delirium. These well-publicized Chicano victories over the entrenched white establishment spread with remarkable speed to other Mexican American communities. Besides the ballot box, a parallel metamorphosis was taking place among Chicanos regarding their psychological emancipation from an Anglo political environment that had promoted patronizing dependency and a sense of cultural inferiority. Mexicans had been repeatedly told, for example, that they lacked the cultural suitability and the required political qualities to govern their own affairs. Chicanos had been oppressed in south Texas for generations and repeatedly assured by the Anglo political machines that whites would watch out for their welfare. Doubly shocking was that Mexican American people were forewarned— *threatened* would be a more accurate word—by the Anglo leadership that any electoral challenges to their political dynasties were not in the best interests of their community. In defiance of these admonitions, the Mexican American community made valiant attempts over the years to unlock the political shackles imposed by Anglo leadership. Each of these courageous efforts against these untruthful ideas of justice resulted in the gradual wearing down of this subservient habit of mind. The electoral uprisings by La Raza Unida Party had considerably eroded a large part of this colonial mentality. This gradual form of psychological emancipation from political racism was not as easy to measure at the time as counting the actual number of seats by La Raza Unida Party, yet in the long term is was critical in the overall quest for political independence.

There is no doubt that the victories in south Texas were the emotional high point of the history of La Raza Unida Party. As a consequence, the political spotlight on Crystal City soon widened as La Raza Unida state chapters were quickly established throughout the Southwest and the Midwest regions. In Colorado, for example, La Raza Unida Party held a political conference in April 1970. Many of those attending had been Democrats for many years but finally became tired of listening to false promises. La Raza Unida in Colorado sponsored several regional conferences and developed a statewide platform addressing the issues of housing, education, economic opportunities, job development, law enforcement, and the redistribution of wealth. In New Mexico, organizers throughout the state met in July 1972 to start a chapter of La Raza Unida. La Raza Unida in New Mexico ran several candidates and launched a voter registration drive for qualifying the party on the statewide ballot. In California, La Raza Unida Party can be traced back to 1970, when several groups called for the establishment of a third party. More important, La Raza Unida Party in California was seen as the political engine that united the diverse Mexican American community. There were also dozens of La Raza Unida Party statewide conferences in the midwestern region of the United States, covering several critical issues and concerns.

Until recently, La Raza Unida Party was generally viewed as nothing more than a political flash in the pan. After all, when compared with the League of United Latin American Citizens, the G.I. Forum, the Mexican American Legal and Defense Fund, and other national organizations, La Raza Unida's lifespan was extremely short. Also, the contributions of La Raza Unida have often taken a backseat to other Chicano movement activities during this time, including the farmworker struggle, student walkouts, and the antiwar movement. As a consequence, La Raza Unida has been denied its rightful place in the annals of community organizations. In retrospect, La Raza Unida Party introduced and fast-forwarded a progressive agenda and strategy, including the titanic struggle to dethrone both major parties inside the Mexican American community. Its broad criticism of the the two-party system was unequivocally fierce. In its short moment of political glory, La Raza Unida compelled Democrats and Republicans to reassess their electoral relationship with Mexican American community, and vice versa.

As a consequence, several of La Raza Unida's issues found their way into the platforms of the major parties. No doubt the Republicans and Democrats understood the political exigency in making certain tactical concessions to the Mexican American community, especially during the 1972, 1974, and 1976 national elections. Another Herculean tack of La Raza Unida was trying to rid the American political system of this legalized white supremacy in the form of obstructive electoral codes and laws. In spite of long odds, La Raza Unida, along with several other organizations, was adamant and eventually successful in ensuring the inclusion of Chicanos under the Voting Rights Act of 1975. A greater contribution of La Raza Unida was to shatter the less-than-flattering myth of the "sleeping giant"—the arrogant assumption that Mexican Americans were politically passive. This myth was largely laid to rest because of the gung-ho temperament of the party.

La Raza Unida Party also came upon the political stage at the exact time when Chicanos were quickly losing faith in the political system. La Raza Unida's arrival was a political boon to the community because it helped mobilize thousands of disillusioned youth back into the political arena, especially after the heart-wrenching deaths of Robert Kennedy and Martin Luther King Jr. Unlike both major parties, La Raza Unida legitimately offered Chicano youth a fulfilling sense of political righteousness and an espirit de corps regarding community service. Countless Chicanos had their political baptism within La Raza Unida and learned firsthand the refined art of grassroots organizing. The party also provided politically sophisticated Chicanos with a unique opportunity to sharpen their already exceptional organizational skill. This varied mix of political minds, however, foreshadowed problems for La Raza Unida.

The Decline of La Raza Unida Party
Tragically, the innocent optimism and enormous potential of La Raza Unida Party quickly faded, and within three years the

meteoric rise of the party was a distant memory. It didn't even survive its political infancy. La Raza Unida Party had offered more promising possibilities for translating the concept of self-determination into political actuality, but it failed, by any measure, to do so. The swift demobilization of La Raza Unida Party can be directly attributed to a fatal combination of external and internal factors.

A critical reason for the traumatic disintegration of La Raza Unida Party was that is never conquered the destructive external forces from outside the community during a disturbing chapter in American political history. Political racism against La Raza Unida was precociously sophisticated, including obstructive electoral and campaign laws, and unrelenting barrage of negative propaganda, financial exhaustion, and unlawful political sabotage. The two major parties and their powerful allies, for instance, successfully masterminded merciless roadblocks against the political dreams of the Mexican American community, including racial gerrymandering, filing fees, candidate fees, at-large district systems, and citizenship and language requirements. In addition, the mass media, politicians from both parties, and their Mexican American yes-man orchestrated a shameful campaign in discrediting La Raza Unida Party by employing Red-baiting tactics and verbally assaulting its membership as nothing more than nationalistic fanatics. Certain sectors of the mass media went to great lengths to prey upon the jingoistic fears and racist paranoia against La Raza Unida in particular and the Chicano civil rights movement in general.

Moreover, La Raza Unida simply did not have the monetary resources required to defeat the Democratic and Republican parties. La Raza Unida Party suffered, for example, from the grinding fatigue of perpetually raising funds for office rent, telephone bills, the cost of campaigning, and other expenses. La Raza Unida Party could not compete with the nearly unlimited amounts of money pouring into the Republican and Democratic parties. There is no doubt that these factors took a heavy political, public relations, and financial toll on La Raza Unida Party and ultimately contributed to its deterioration.

Over and above these political, media, and legal burdens, however, was a far more sinister source of unlawful action against La Raza Unida Party. The powerful cartels of government and their corporate allies ominously viewed La Raza Unida Party as a subversive threat to the national security of the United States. (During the Nixon administration, for example, Secretary of State Henry Kissinger had his staff investigate Chicano nationalism and its possible consequences for the United States.) Thus, La Raza Unida Party's ultranationalist demands for the nullification of the Treaty of Guadalupe Hidalgo and the territorial settlement of the Southwest were seen by the highest levels of U.S. power as the dangerous "Quebec" within its national borders. La Raza Unida's philosophy of radical nationalism was viewed as a racial knife ripping apart society's political fabric.

These were not idle fears by those in control of the Anglo power structure. The astonishing political takeover of Crystal City, Texas; the unexpected armed rebellion in Tierra Amarilla, New Mexico, over land rights; and the massive student walkouts in East Los Angeles reaffirmed their anxiety that La Raza Unida could eventually stir up the greater national Mexican American community. Moreover, there was even governmental speculation that Chicanos and Mexicans were co-conspirators plotting to bring about the reunification of the Southwest with Mexico. The popular tide of Chicano nation building resulted in clandestine government operations designed to destroy La Raza Unida Party at any cost, thus obliterating any hopes of a Chicano homeland.

Because the causes of political reaction are both real and imaginary, it is hard to distinguish where one ends and the other starts. This much is known, however: The governmental ambush against La Raza Unida included such surreptitious activities as wiretapping and break-ins at La Raza Unida Party headquarters; widespread surveillance, intimidation, and questionable arrests by law enforcement agencies; mean-spirited attempts by state officials to inactivate La Raza Unida Party leaders; bribes, disguised as grants, offered by both major political parties; infiltration by government undercover agents; and other unsavory tactics of political skullduggery. There is no question that these measures contributed to La Raza Unida Party's rapid decline.

More painful still was the somber truth that La Raza Unida Party contributed to its own swift demise due to a succession of internal blunders and embarrassing political missteps. First and foremost, from its inception La Raza Unida Party was plagued with sexism, which severely tarnished its image in the eyes of many Chicanas and their male allies. La Raza Unida was a patriarchal institution with a male-centered agenda. With rare exceptions, the majority of Chicanas were given only minor roles and were generally ignored whenever they offered valuable suggestions concerning the direction of the party. Inasmuch as women were the political backbone of numerous local and state chapters, too many men within the party still perceived chicanas as political competitors instead of compatriots. La Raza Unida Party's propaganda declared that *la familia* was the most crucial political unit in the community—its posters and flyers depicted a man, woman, and child with the bold words *La Raza Unida*. But this portrayal, with the male as head of the family, unsurprisingly spilled into the political arena in the mythical image of man as the sole breadwinner.

Regardless of their reasons, most of the male leadership cautiously favored their own political collateral over that of the community's larger interests by failing to unselfishly mentor and support a critical mass of women. The result was that women were infuriated and compelled to form their own caucus within the party structure. But this division within the party did not help women, and as a consequence of this political straitjacket, several key Chicanas left the party feeling like political exiles. The clear contradiction here was that while men in La Raza Unida Party demanded political freedom from the larger society, they closed the political doors of equal opportunity to Chicanas and failed to comprehend the vital link between feminism and nationalism from a historical and community standpoint. This broader perspective would have revealed that women's rights are linked to civil rights and that the most successful political movements have been those where women and men were co-leaders. There is no question that the infusion of women into leadership positions of the party would have strengthened the party's capabilities in achieving some of its goals, despite the political interference from the outside. Moreover by depicting the Mexican family as husband, wife, and child, the leadership of La Raza Unida Party unintentionally promoted deep-rooted homophobia and inadvertently politically alienated other (nontraditional) households within the Mexican American community.

The second major contradiction of La Raza Unida Party was that its leaders viewed themselves as ethnic revolutionists and secessionists boycotting the two-party system, when in actuality they accepted the status quo of the two-party system by conducting voter registration drives, hosting conventions, endorsing candidates, and engaging in other standard Anglo electoral behavior. Indeed, the electoral efforts of La Raza Unida Party proved to be a double-edged sword, helping to further legitimize and, consequently, make stronger the same political system it was trying to overthrow. Without doubt, this oversimplified illusion of the electoral process revealed a profound ignorance by the party about the true nature of the American political system. A case in point was the intensive voter registration effort for qualifying the party on the state ballot. La Raza Unida Party signed up thousands and thousands of people to vote, ostensibly for its candidates. Yet, contrary to La Raza Unida's strategy, thousands of these new voters also cast their votes for the much-despised Democrats and Republicans. Unintentionally, La Raza Unida's reformist strategies, to some extent, helped politically resuscitate and vindicate the Democrats and Republicans at a time when these two parties were under ferocious condemnation both on the home front and from abroad.

Furthermore, La Raza Unida Party's overriding preoccupation with short-term political campaigns, resulting in devastating defeats at the polls, damaged its ability to invest in grassroots organizing for the long haul. These electoral setbacks were direct-

ly linked to the party's miscalculation regarding the initial victories in south Texas. Soon after these successful elections, especially in Crystal City, party organizers elsewhere prematurely
attempted to replicate the "Crystal City model" in the urban
areas, with the belief that the great numbers of Mexican
Americans could overwhelm the traditional political, and demographic nature of each Mexican community. While it is true that
Mexican Americans have much in common wherever they reside
in the United States, there is also the political reality of diverse
political environments that require distinctive strategies for social
change. This belated revelation regarding La Raza Unida Party's
electoral overreach led to a string of demoralizing defeats at the
polls and created a sense of political disorientation that soon
diminished the community's lofty expectations of the party.

The longing to renew its cultural bond exclusively with
Mexico also created immense problems for La Raza Unida. La
Raza Unida Party's political role models, for example, were the
Aztecs and Mexico's revolutionary heroes. Ethnic purism can be
awkward and confusing, as La Raza Unida soon discovered. This
narrow selectivity in terms of political forbears dramatized the
party's confusion regarding the political dimensions of ethnicity, nationality, and race throughout most of Central and Latin
America, and thus prevented La Raza Unida Party from establishing powerful alliances with non-Mexican Latino groups.

In connection with this cultural and racial dilemma, La
Raza Unida Party never made it abundantly clear what would
physically happen to non-Mexican people residing in the
Southwest once Aztlan was achieved. Would these individuals be
deported, segregated, integrated, assimilated, incarcerated, exter-
minated, or what? Also La Raza Unida leaders were not crystal
clear regarding their approach to achieving an independent
homeland. Would it be attained by purchase, nonviolence,
armed rebellion, or with the support of global allies? The lack of
thoughtful contingency plans regarding the political status of
non-Mexican people and the strategic means for acquiring geographical autonomy raised serious doubts regarding La Raza
Unida Party's competence in carrying out its political mission.

La Raza Unida likewise suffered immensely by failing to acknowledge and properly learn from the genealogy of community organizations that preceded it. By seeking its political strength and spiritual guidance mainly from the Aztecs, Emiliano Zapata, and Pancho Villa, La Raza Unida almost never gave its due respect and credit to the political pioneers who had come immediately before it and who had painfully laid the political groundwork for the Chicano generation. Forgetting their rich political history in the United States was a fatal mistake and led to condescending to the community's gritty past. La Raza Unida Party was not the political exception to the historical rule, as it had believed, but the natural political heir to a long and rich continuum of peaceful reform movements inside the Mexican American community. The political shortsightedness of La Raza Unida Party in truly recognizing its inherited reformist nature and justly crediting previous generations contributed directly to numerous organizational problems and its eventual downfall.

Instead, La Raza Unida leadership chose to paint previous Mexican American movements and organizations as too politically traditional and obedient to the two major parties. La Raza Unida activists pointed at the organizations put together by earlier generations—groups such as the League of United Latin American Citizens (LULAC), the G.I. Forum, the Mexican American Political Association (MAPA), the Political Association of Spanish-Speaking Organizations, and the "Viva Kennedy" Clubs—and argued that these self-proclaimed power brokers were overly eager to compromise on issues where they should have stood firm. In addition, La Raza Unida pointed out that these Mexican American groups had played by the rules of Anglo politics and had very little to show for their flustered efforts.

Additionally, La Raza Unida Party accused the community advocates of assimilation and of committing ethnic treason against their own people by not supporting a separatist position. True, there were some self-centered leaders who had prostituted their ethnicity for token positions within both major parties. In order to gain further political credibility, these opportunists unfairly attacked La Raza Unida Party leaders as demagogues and soapbox Communists preaching racial hate and ethnic balkanization. Yet these same self-serving detractors were personally reaping political benefits from La Raza Unida's pressure on both parties to improve the lot of Mexican Americans. Nevertheless, La Raza Unida's political indictment of prior generations backfired and harmed its ability to mobilize the entire community because it did not take full advantage of the rich experience of older leaders yearning to lend their genuine support and vast expertise. Although La Raza Unida Party appeared to have captivated the youthful heart and soul within the community, in reality it had only a small cadre of devoted followers, comprised largely of impatient college students. Thus, rather than becoming an authentic united front with a broader and wiser cross-section of their political predecessors, La Raza Unida Party unnecessarily infuriated Mexican American community leaders by engaging in this high-risk strategy, and eventually paid a steep price for its go-it-alone attitude. A better understanding of Mexican American political history would have shown the leadership of La Raza Unida Party that it was both liberated and constrained by its long and complex intergenerational past.

Another contradiction that La Raza Unida Party never resolved was the vexing question of class. La Raza Unida erroneously sought political equality without adequately addressing the fundamental inequality produced by capitalism. While many of the issues in La Raza Unida Party's platform were clearly sympathetic to the Mexican American Working class, the party downplayed Marxism as a useful paradigm for social change. In all fairness, there were elements within La Raza Unida who tried diligently to move the working-class question to the forefront of the race-versus-class debate. Without question, these intense ideological arguments regarding the seniority of race or class created highly charged divisions within the party. In the end, the party leadership chose to keep itself at arm's length from Marxism and—as was the case with women—advocates of class consciousness were prevented from having their voices heard. This injurious lack of focus by the party on class impaired its ability to closely examine Marxism as part of the social equation for Chicano liberation.

As a result, the party leadership mischaracterized the oppression of Chicanos essentially as racist. But even if they had defeated racism, or thought they did, Chicanos cannot acquire self-determination and political equality within the framework of a capitalist state, since capitalism is intrinsically a system of unequal power that thrives on sexism, racism, classism, and other "isms." The consolidation of power, wealth, and prestige by a few—including a handful of lucky Chicanos—inevitably results in social discrepancies in education, health care, justice, housing, and political influence. Since capitalism is based on the centralization of power and the social dependency of the working class on the rich, Chicano self-determination cannot be righteously achieved inside this type of profit system. This basic economic fact of life was generally misunderstood by the leadership of La Raza Unida Party and led, in large part, to its political meltdown.

This class discrepancy in wealth and power explains in large part why the upsurge in political visibility among a handful of Mexican Americans today has not translated into social and economic upward mobility for the majority of working-class Mexican Americans. Ironically, both the record-breaking numbers of Mexican American legislators in positions of prestige and responsibility and an energized voter base in the community have been matched by an ever-increasing number of attacks on bilingual education, affirmative action programs, and immigrants. The root of this contradiction does not rest on the broad shoulders of these Mexican American lawmakers and voters who are staking claim to their fair share of the political terrain. Rather, this societal antithesis is the result of Chicanos formulating their political agendas inside an unequal economic system.

Another painful predicament for La Raza Unida Party was that it never reconciled its quest of ideological purity with its democratic respect for divergent political perspectives. La Raza Unida viewed itself as a democratic organization and welcomed a patchwork of both political neophytes and savvy veterans into its ranks. As a result of this open-door recruitment policy, the party consisted of a hodgepodge of divergent needs, varied opinions, and numerous viewpoints regarding the party's mission, goals, and ideology. One disagreeable aspect of this odd mixture of activists was that the party was organizationally unmanageable, largely unfocused, and lacked any consensus regarding priority issues.

Another effect was that the party soon fell into an internecine struggle that virtually paralyzed it. As with most organizations, several key individuals percolated to the top of the party's leadership and became partisans of various political cliques that quickly overshadowed the core mission and issues of the party. There is nothing more destructive in politics than unthinking devotion to leaders, and political skirmishes soon broke out within La Raza Unida. There were some members who implored the party leadership to find common ground, but their passionate pleas for unity fell on uncooperative ears. Unfortunately, many rank-and-file members were eventually forced to sacrifice their moral principle of reconciliation in exchange for a cultlike ideology.

The ultimate tragedy of this "patron" syndrome was that it took place just as the party was hosting its first national convention in El Paso, Texas, in 1972. Behind the scenes, a frightening turn ensued as intermediaries from the various camps masterminded attempts to stampede the gathering on behalf of their respective leaders. In a last-ditch effort, a handful of delegates had come to the convention on a peacemaking mission. Still and all, in the end, very few participants stayed above the fray. On the last day of the convention, the top leaders of the party emotionally clenched and raised their fists as a communal symbol of unity and political fanfare. But this public display of compatibility was a masquerade, because the infighting continued immediately after the convention. This organization quarrel further polarized most of the party faithful as they gravitated into tightly knit groups. Too, dissent after the convention wasted much time and energy, leaving La Raza Unida fragmented and ineffective in organizing new chapters and providing much-needed services to the community.

Perhaps more distressing was the party's failure in the art of compromise, thoroughly contrary to the principles of community democracy and honest political disagreement. Rather than finding a political niche for everyone's talents and skills, the party splintered into a myriad of feuding factions. There was even the unfortunate suggestion by fervent hard-liners about creating a new Chicano party in competition with La Raza Unida Party—a grossly offensive echo of the two-party system that La Raza Unida was supposedly fighting against in the first place. In the end, it became clear that the unity of the party had been damaged beyond repair, evidenced by the various factions increasing their attempts to purge their opponents from the organization. La Raza Unida Party never recovered from this political tailspin.

This nationwide conflict among the high-profile leadership of La Raza Unida Party also ricocheted into the internal affairs of local and state chapters. It exacerbated the already long-held suspicions and widespread disdain between the local and national governing bodies of the party. The party leadership initially failed to foresee and resolve the competition between its local chapters and the national ruling body, *El Congreso del Partido de la Raza Unida*. This ongoing struggle for political turf and an unwillingness on the part of both centralization and advocates of local control to find common ground indelibly marred La Raza Unida Party.

By the mid-1970s, La Raza Unida Party was merely a political shell of itself, despite a final attempt to jump-start the party by announcing La Raza Unida Party candidates for governor in Texas and California in 1974. With its political voice all but negligible, the eleventh-hour gesture was more an anticlimactic act of political desperation than one of boldness. Soon disillusioned members began leaving the party and scattering throughout the political landscape. Some former members of La Raza Unida became born-again Democrats; a few joined the GOP; others joined leftist parties; and yet others became involved with a variety of pressing issues, including reapportionment and immigrant rights. As a result of this leadership dispersion, echoes of La Raza Unida Party's political influence were soon found in many community organizations throughout the United States. Still there were pockets of die-hard La Raza Unida party organizers operating in the community as late as the 1980's.

Conclusion
The mythology of La Raza Unida Party can become irritatingly sentimental and oversimplified. The line between symbolism and substance is a precarious one. More troublesome is that political fantasy can lead to smug complacency. This article has attempted to demystify La Raza Unida Party by presenting a balanced assessment of its rightful place in the chronicles of Mexican American political history. It is especially important for the next generation of leaders to learn this story by heart and to draw lessons from the party's strengths and weaknesses. La Raza Unida Party's Political mishaps cannot be allowed to outweigh its mighty contributions, nor can the party be dismissed simply as a political tantrum.

Its feisty spirit established new views and fresh approaches to looking at social change. For a few glorious years, La Raza Unida Party took center stage in the community as it labored tirelessly in expanding political and social opportunities, cultural legitimacy, and extracting economic resources for the community. As a consequence, La Raza Unida Party altered, transformed, and elevated the political standards for future generations of Mexican Americans. Its groundbreaking work, for instance, paved the way for the eventual election of the current crop of Mexican American legislators, who to this day have never publicly acknowledged their political debt to La Raza Unida Party. The dedicated members of La Raza Unida Party were not martyrs but ordinary community folks who performed extraordinary acts of courage in their odyssey for social justice, ethnic affirmation, and political validity. They charitably gave all that was humanly possible for a better quality of life for the masses. And, like all mortals, they had their flaws.

Meanwhile, the period following the 1996 presidential election has again witnessed the Democrats and Republicans trying to make amends to the Mexican American community for not paying enough attention to their issues in that election. Once more, both parties are engaged in a political courtship for 1998 and 2000. The Democrats, for example, are shamelessly meeting with their handful of Mexican American cronies, while the GOP has failed to make good on its pledges to forsake its outrageous reputation as the party of white privilege. Both parties are currently supporting regressive policies and ballot measures that are clearly anti-Mexican American. Their transparent speechifying and legislative trickery are solely designed to hide the fact that they want to have it both ways. Political babble camouflaged as political sincerity cannot legitimately substitute for thoughtful social policies and effective remedies. The key question today is not whether the Mexican American community needs an alternative to the counterfeit nature of the two-party system, but what new form this will take. Is the political reincarnations of La Raza Unida Party the correct response to the current reactionary forces of resentment, prejudice, hate, and fear? The practical answer is no.

But neither is the current group of elected and appointed Mexican American bureaucrats the answer either. The unavoidable truth is that most of them seem to be politically marooned in the past and lack the headstrong courage required to challenge the reactionary agendas of both major parties. A handful of newly elected officials appear to have the political backbone to wage this fight, but the majority of don't-rock-the-boat representatives are in deep confusion and lack the community's confidence that they can solve pressing problems. Right now, things look extraordinarily bleak regarding this wishy-washy leadership. More than ever, the Mexican American community needs a new set of perceptive leaders, diverse organizations, grassroots strategies, broader coalitions, and assorted visions. This type of competent leadership can no longer afford to waste valuable time debating the what-if scenarios regarding La Raza Unida Party or engaging in male chauvinism and invidious ethnocentrism.

Short of a political miracle, community restructuring requires a new set of forward-looking leaders who can put together a strong and mature political base—a new political building block on top of the building blocks already set in place by La Raza Unida Party and the current political leadership. This step-by-step political discovery about the true meaning of leadership has several key parts. First, the new leadership must be a cooperative partnership between women and men; second, the new leadership must reach out and embrace non-Mexican Latino groups; third, it must incorporate the full range of community experiences by stretching out to lesbians and gays, the disabled, senior citizens, and disenfranchised youth; fourth, it must establish long-term alliances with other people of color, unions, church groups, sympathetic Euro-Americans, and global allies; fifth, it must be confident enough to hear and then act upon unpopular beliefs; sixth, it must fearlessly address the economic causes that led to the formation of an underclass in which women, Latinos, and other people of color are represented in disproportionate numbers; seventh, it must at last break its bondage to the two-party system; eighth, it must remain above the petty politics in the community; and finally, the new leadership must have a strong knowledge of its political and historical roots.

This last recommendation is crucial to the overall political survival and social betterment of the community. Simultaneously moving forward and looking backward to one's political ancestors for guidance both is possible and provides a truer sense of the future, including political hazards. Each generation of Mexican Americans in its own way has politically confronted and persevered in the face of unspeakable social obstacles, including horrendous living conditions, flagrant disrespect for their civil rights, and a profound betrayal by the larger society. The Mexican American leadership has been unflinching in its struggle against prejudice and discrimination. By gradually peeling away another layer of racism, each generation opened the door of opportunity wider for the next generation to walk through. This dialectical process is analogous to a political relay race where each generation hands the baton to the next generation of leaders; ultimately, they all win as a team. Moreover, this generational kinship has reflected several common themes, including an unshakable belief in the essence of charity, spiritual pride, a yearning for justice, boundless optimism, a profound compassion for the community's elders, and unquestioning self-sacrifice for the benefit of the next generation. This partnership of generations had undeniably left its mark on the social, economic, intellectual, and cultural landscape of this country.

This complex and rich political heritage will benefit the new leadership tremendously and keep it one step ahead of society's antidemocratic forces. Political equality for Mexican Americans and other socially alienated groups, however, is not their sole responsibility. The larger Anglo society also has a moral obligation to eradicate state-sponsored oppression by swaying public opinion to the side of justice and equality—and has a political stake in doing so. As the community approaches this new political horizon, the forthcoming generation of Mexican American leaders will inherit a rare opportunity to rejuvenate the nation and move it toward real democracy. By effectively incorporating these political recommendations and many others, the new leadership will build the broad-based alliance needed to bring about the institutional change required for true social justice for all.

Recommended Readings

This bibliography is by no means exhaustive. Rather, it provides the reader with a cross-section of research that contributed to the overall spirit of this article.

Calderon, Jose. "Reflections of La Raza Unida Party." Paper presented at the annual meeting of the National Association for Chicano Studies, Sacramento, California, April 13, 1985.

Garcia, Armando R. "Institutional Completeness and La Raza Unida Party." In *Chicanos and Native Americans*, edited by Rudolph O. de la Garza,

Anthony Kruszewski, and Tomás A. Arciniega. Englewood Cliffs, New Jersey: Prentice-Hall, 1973.

García, Ignacio M. *United We Win: The Rise and Fall of La Raza Unida Party.* Tucson: Mexican American Studies and Research Center, University of Arizona, 1989.

Garcia, Richard. "The Chicano Movement and the Mexican American Community, 1972–1978: An Interpretive Essay." *Socialist Review* 8 (1978): 124–27.

Gutierrez, Armando G., and Herbert Hirsch. "Political Maturation and Political Awareness: The Case of the Crystal City Chicano." *Aztlan* 5 (1974).

Gutierrez, Jose Angel. "La Raza and Revolution: The Empirical Conditions for Revolution in Four South Texas Counties." Master's thesis, St. Mary's University, San Antonio, Texas, 1968.

————. "Chicanos and Mexicans Under Surveillance: 1940–1980," *Renato Rosaldo Lecture Series* monograph no. 2, edited by Ignacia Garcia. Tucson: Mexican American Studies and Research Center, University of Arizona, 1986.

Juarez, Alberto. "The Emergence of El Partido de la Raza Unida: California's New Chicano Party." *Aztlan* 3 (1973).

Miller, Michael V. "Chicano Community Control in South Texas: Problems and Prospects." *Journal of Ethnic Studies* 3 (1975): 70–89.

Muñoz, Carlos, Jr., and Mario Barrera. "La Raza Unida Party and the Chicano Student Movement in California." *Social Science Journal* 19 (April 1982).

Navarro, Armando. "El Partido de la Raza Unida: A Peaceful Revolution." Ph.D. dissertation, University of California, Riverside, 1974.

————. *Mexican American Youth Organization: Avant-Garde of the Chicano Movement in Texas.* Austin: University of Texas Press, 1996.

————. *The Cristal Experiment: A Chicano Struggle for Community Control.* Madison: The University of Wisconsin Press, 1998.

Santillan, Richard. "The Politics of Cultural Nationalism: El Partido de La Raza Unida in Southern California, 1969–1978." Ph.D. dissertation, Claremont Graduate School, 1978.

Shockley, John Staples. *Chicano Revolt in a Texas Town.* Notre Dame, IN: University of Notre Dame Press, 1974.

Sosa, Riddle Adaljisa. "Chicano and El Moviemiento." *Aztlan* 5 (1974): 155–65.

Swadesh, Francis L. "The Alianza Movement: Catalyst for Social Change in New Mexico." In *Chicano: The Beginnings of Bronze Power,* edited by Renato Rosaldo, Robert A. Calvert, and Gustav L. Seligmann. New York: William Morrow, 1974.

Tirado, Miguel David. "Mexican American Community Political Organizations: The Key to Chicano Political Power." *Aztlan* 1 (1970): 53–78.

Notes on Contributors

Luis Aponte-Parés is Associate Professor of Community Planning at the University of Massachusetts, Boston. A lifelong activist in the Puerto Rican community, he has worked on planning, housing, and community development. Two areas are central to his research: how Puerto Rican and Latino history intersects the changing urban landscapes in the United States and representation of Latino identity in the urban milieu. Recent publications include an article on *casitas* in *Places,* an environmental design journal, and an essay in *The Puerto Rican Movement: Voices from the Diaspora.*

Edna Bonacich is Professor of Sociology and Ethnic Studies at the University of California, Riverside. Her work has mainly focused on issues of race and class. She coedited a book on the apparel industry in the Pacific Rim, entitled *Global Production,* and is now working on a coauthored volume on the Los Angeles garment industry. For almost 10 years, she has been working as a volunteer with UNITE (Union of Needletrade, Industrial and Textile Employees).

Teresa Córdova is Associate Professor of Community and Regional Planning at the University of New Mexico. She works closely with the Environmental Justice Movement and is a member of the Southwest Organizing Project and a former member of the Subcommittee on Hazardous Waste and Facility Siting of the National Environmental Justice Council of the EPA. Dr. Córdova also publishes in the area of Chicana studies. She is Executive Director of the Resource Center for Raza Planning, a group of research activists engaged in research and policy analysis on issues affecting traditional communities in New Mexico.

Martha E. Gimenez is Associate Professor of Sociology at the University of Colorado at Boulder. She is originally from Argentina, where she studied law and sociology at the Universidad Nacional de Cordoba. She has published numerous articles and book chapters on Marxist population theory, Marxist feminist theory, poverty, and the politics of racial/ethnic construction.

Gilbert G. González is Professor in the School of Social Sciences and Chicano Latino Studies at the University of California, Irvine. His publications include *Chicano Education in the Era of Segregation and Labor and Community: Mexican Citrus Workers in a Southern California County, 1900–1950*. His forthcoming study examines the political interventions of the Mexican consulates into the expatriate community between 1920 and 1940.

George Katsiaficas is Professor in the School of Social Sciences at Wentworth Institute of Technology, the editor of *New Political Science,* and the author of *The Imagination of the New Left: A Global Analysis of 1968,* as well as *The Subversion of Politics: European Autonomous Social Movements and the Decolonization of Everyday Life.* The latter book won the 1998 Michael Harrington Award of the American Political Science Association's Section for a New Political Science.

Victor M. Rodriguez is Professor of Sociology and member of the Social Science Division at Concordia University in Irvine, California. He writes columns and journalistic pieces in Spanish and English on Puerto Rican/Latino issues for a number of publications and has been interviewed on Latino issues by national news organizations, including radio and television. He also is an antiracism trainer and board member of Crossroads Ministry, a national interfaith racial justice organization.

Richard Santillan is Professor of Ethnic and Women's Studies at California State Polytechnic University at Pomona. Dr. Santillan has published extensively on Chicano/a political history, voting rights, and Mexican history in the Midwest. He has recently completed a manuscript entitled *Encuentros y Cuentos: An Oral History of Mexicans in the Midwestern United States, 1900–1950*. Professor Santillan is currently working on a book on the history of La Raza Unida Party in southern California.

Rodolfo D. Torres is Professor of Chicano/Latino Studies and Public Policy at California State University, Long Beach, and Visiting Professor of Educational Policy, University of California, Irvine. He is coeditor of *New American Destinies, Latinos and Education: A Critical Reader, The Latino Studies Reader,* and *Race, Identity, and Citizenship: A Reader,* and coauthor of the forthcoming book *The Latino Metropolis.* He is a member of the editorial board of *New Political Science.*